EMBROIDERY

A MAKER'S GUIDE

EMBROIDERY

A MAKER'S GUIDE

With over 230 photographs and illustrations

Thames & Hudson | V&A

First published in the United Kingdom in 2017
by Thames & Hudson in association with the
Victoria and Albert Museum

Embroidery: A Maker's Guide
© 2017 Victoria and Albert Museum, London/
Thames & Hudson Ltd, London

V&A images © 2017 Victoria and Albert Museum, London
Illustrations and project photography © 2017 Thames &
Hudson Ltd, London
Text and layout © 2017 Thames & Hudson Ltd, London

See also Picture Credits p.176

Design by Hyperkit
Illustrations by Eleanor Crow
Projects commissioned by Amy Christian
Project editing by Faye Robson
Project photography by We Are Studio

British Library Cataloguing-in-Publication Data
A catalogue record for this book is available from
the British Library

ISBN 978-0-500-29327-0

Printed and bound in China by Toppan Leefung
Printing Limited

To find out about all our publications, please visit
www.thamesandhudson.com. There you can subscribe
to our e-newsletter, browse or download our current
catalogue, and buy any titles that are in print.

Frontispiece: 'Acanthus' wall hanging (detail), c.1880
(designed by William Morris 1878)
Felted woollen cloth embroidered with silks,
249.5 x 169.3 cm (98¼ x 66⅝ in.)
V&A: T.66–1939

Back cover images (clockwise, from top left):
Kimono (detail), 1890–1930
Plain-weave ramie with a stitched cotton design,
128 x 100 cm (50⅜ x 39⅜ in.)
V&A: FE.141–1983

'Acanthus' wall hanging (detail), c.1880
(designed by William Morris 1878)
Felted woollen cloth embroidered with silks,
249.5 x 169.3 cm (98¼ x 66⅝ in.)
V&A: T.66–1939

Sleeve panel (detail), 1610–20
Linen embroidered with silk thread, 61.5 x 21.5 cm
(24¼ x 8½ in.)
V&A: T.11–1950

Border for a woman's dress (detail), 19th century
Muslin embroidered with beetle wings and gold wire,
117 x 33 cm (46 x 13 in.)
V&A: IS.468–1992

Skirt (detail), c.1880
Satin-weave silk embroidered with silk thread
and *shisha*, 201 x 86.5 cm (79⅛ x 34 in.)
V&A: IS.2304–1883

Waistcoat (detail), 1630–40
Linen embroidered with wool thread,
51.5 x 32 cm (20¼ x 12½ in.; across shoulders)
V&A: T.843–1974

V&A Publishing

Supporting the world's leading
museum of art and design,
the Victoria and Albert
Museum, London

EMBROIDERY TODAY

James Merry is a hand-embroidery artist from Gloucestershire, England, now based in Iceland. He works from a small cabin on a lake outside of Reykjavík, working by hand in a variety of media.

Hand embroidery has been enjoying something of a revival in recent years. As with any craft boasting such a rich and long history, it naturally becomes the task for each generation to rediscover and redefine the medium on its own terms. That this resurgence should happen now comes as no surprise. In a world saturated with decades of quick, disposable mass production, it is only logical that people might find a new appreciation for handicraft – placing value firmly back on precision, quality and originality.

There is an inherent personality to hand embroidery that can never be replicated by a machine; they are as different as a page of printed text and a handwritten letter. While everything around us seems to be getting faster and more homogenized, and time becomes our most valuable currency, a renewed regard for and enjoyment of hand embroidery seems not only inevitable, but necessary.

The upsurge of interest in embroidery can be witnessed across a range of disciplines: as an ever-more-prevalent feature on the catwalks and in couture; with a more therapeutic application in social initiatives such as the charity Fine Cell Work, which takes embroidery into prisons for the purposes of rehabilitation. In the past, grand embroidery commissions may have come from imperial or royal courts – now, Hollywood studios fill that role, putting many craftspeople to work on intricate costumes for fantastical or historical film and television.

As is to be expected with such an ancient and traditional craft, embroidery comes with its own host of associations (domestic, regal, military, feminine, ecclesiastical, etc.), which make it susceptible to some wonderfully unexpected subversions. For myself and many other contemporary embroiderers, this seems to be exactly what makes it such a seductive craft to work in at the moment. My ongoing series of hand-embroidered sportswear and my headpieces for the musician Björk (see opposite) play upon specific dualities, expressed through the medium itself: machine- and handmade, urban and rural, masculine and feminine, human and animal. The satisfying juxtaposition of tradition and cutting-edge technology is something I have also been interested to explore through my work, using modern materials (latex and plastics, embroidered with light-sensitive threads) alongside established techniques such as goldwork, silk shading and beading.

It is particularly pleasing for me to see that the language and imagery associated with embroidery is suddenly to be found everywhere in modern life. Words traditionally associated with needlework now permeate digital and scientific language – we talk of email threads, strands of DNA, the web, the net, and now, most satisfying of them all, string theory. An embroiderer will identify immediately with the idea that the universe and its contents are made up of sub-atomic loops and threads.

To admire a piece of hand embroidery is to appreciate time itself – your fingertips can almost touch the hours, days and weeks embedded in every stitch. I urge the readers of this book to relish the relaxing pace that the medium requires. This pace and the attention to detail needed can be the perfect antidote to the distractions of modern life. The projects presented here will introduce you to core embroidery techniques – nurturing a focus, patience and precision that I hope will be as rewarding to you as the finished pieces themselves.

James Merry, *Nike/Eyrarrós*, 2016

Meredith Woolnough,
Spring Leaves (machine
embroidery), 2016

Björk & James Merry, 'Moth' mask, 2015

Tessa Perlow, *Mixed Wildflower Hoop*, 2016

Tirelli Costumi (to a design by Massimo
Cantini Parrini), detail of a costume
for the King of Strongcliff, played
by Vincent Cassell in the 2015 film
Il racconto dei racconti (Tale of Tales)

A Chanel seamstress
puts the final touches
to the Chanel Haute
Couture Fall/Winter
2006 collection in the
Chanel workshop above
rue Cambon, Paris, 2006

Jenny King (design), by a Fine Cell Work stitcher, 'Moustaches' cushion, 2009. Fine Cell Work is a UK-based social enterprise that trains prisoners in paid, skilled, creative needlework.

Christian Dior, ready-to-wear womenswear Spring/Summer 2017, on the runway at Paris Fashion Week, 2016

Manish Arora, womenswear Spring/Summer 2017, on the runway at Paris Fashion Week, 2016

TOOLS & MATERIALS

Specialist shops and online retailers can supply today's embroiderer with any number of gadgets and a vast range of threads and background fabrics, but you need only a few essential items to get started. In this chapter we provide information about useful equipment and widely used materials. But what you need is listed with each project, so check exactly what you require rather than buying everything at once. The projects featured here also mention stitches, some of which may be new to you. Consult the stitch guide on pp.14-17 if you're not familiar with any of the named techniques.

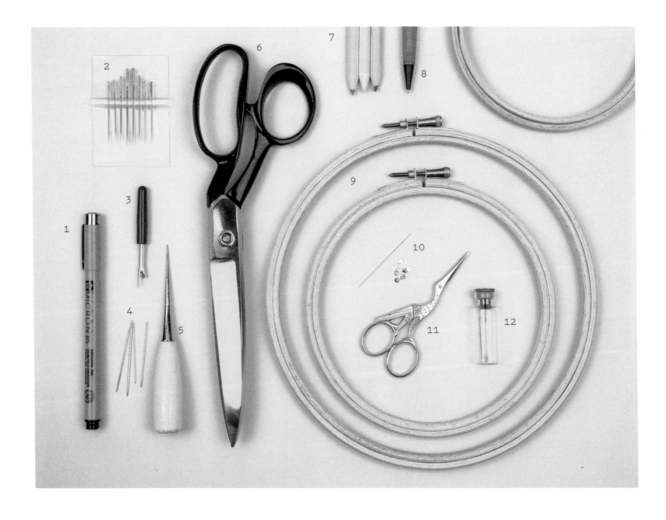

Markers

There is a huge range of markers, many intended specifically for fabric; you may wish to experiment to find which you prefer.

Pencils

A propelling (mechanical) pencil (8) is ideal for marking designs on lighter fabrics, as you can draw accurate lines of a constant width. Quilter's pencils (7) – commonly white or silver – stay sharp and are useful for marking on darker fabrics, as are watercolour pencils.

Erasable pens

Air- and water-erasable markers are used for marking lines which you will later want to remove. Air-erasable marks will disappear automatically after a few days. Water-erasable marks are removed by dabbing with a cotton pad dipped in cold water.

Permanent markers

If you wish to make marks that will last, use a permanent pen (1) that contains archival-quality ink (such as a Pigma), as this is resistant to fading from both light exposure and age.

Cutting tools

Scissors

A pair of dressmaking or fabric scissors (6) is required for cutting fabrics. Embroidery or sharp, fine-pointed scissors (11) are needed for cutting threads and for fine detailed cutwork. Keep a separate pair of craft scissors for cutting paper and other non-fabrics, as these materials will ruin the blades of your embroidery scissors.

Other tools

A seam ripper (3), also known as a stitch unpicker, is handy for taking out stitching mistakes. A sharp-pointed tool called a stiletto or tailor's awl (5) is also useful, for piercing holes in cutwork or when working with thick or precious-metal threads.

Pins

General dressmaking pins are fine for most tasks. If you are incorporating appliqué or working on fiddly items, small, sharp appliqué pins are useful, as they can be placed close together, and their little rounded heads prevent threads from getting caught around them when stitching.

Needles for hand sewing

A wide variety of needles is available, sized and shaped for different tasks. Each type of needle also comes in a range of sizes – the higher the number, the smaller and finer the needle. Using the correct high-quality needle makes the job easier and more enjoyable. Needles do get blunt, so replace them regularly.

Sharps (4)

These medium-length, sharp-pointed needles are for general-purpose sewing, and are also ideal for hand appliqué. It is useful to buy a pack of mixed sizes. For finer fabrics, use a smaller (higher number) needle.

Betweens (12)

These are shorter than sharps and easy to control when making small stitches. Often used in hand quilting.

Embroidery/crewel (2)

These needles are like sharps, but they have a longer eye so they can accommodate lightweight (thicker) threads such as stranded cotton.

Tapestry

The large eyes of these needles enable the user to thread tapestry wool and other thick threads and yarns with ease. The blunt point passes through canvas, for example, without damaging the fabric.

Chenille

Like tapestry needles, these have large eyes – useful for thick threads – but they have sharp points for piercing thick, coarse fabrics.

Beading (10)

Beading needles are thin and flexible, with small eyes. Traditionally they are long, but shorter, easier-to-use needles have been created for embroiderers; they are available with both sharp and rounded points.

Hoops

A hoop (9) comprises two concentric rings, circular or oval. Mounting your work between the rings will give you a taut surface on which to stitch, helping you to work even stitches and prevent the fabric from puckering. You can bind one of the rings with bias tape or thin webbing, which will help to keep the tension even and is gentler on your fabric. Don't leave your embroidery in the hoop when not working on it as this will cause creases. Rectangular frames, such as artists' stretcher frames, are useful for large projects.

Machine embroidery

A simple machine is all that's required for most embroidery projects; even entry-level models usually have a range of pre-programmed stitches. Unless you want to incorporate commercial patterns or are interested in using software to create your own designs, you don't need an expensive, computerized embroidery machine. However, a needle-down option is useful, as it enables you to set the machine so that when you stop stitching, the needle finishes in the work, allowing you to change your sewing direction neatly. For free-machine embroidery, you need to lower the machine's feed dogs (the zigzag-shaped teeth that feed the fabric through the machine), or buy a cover for them (you can also use a piece of hard plastic). You may wish to mount your fabric in a hoop to hold it taut; it can also be helpful to use fabric stabilizer (a special material placed against the wrong side of the work) to help prevent puckering.

Presser feet

The presser foot (17) on your machine keeps the fabric flat and holds it in position against the feed dogs so that it doesn't move around when sewing. There are specialized feet for different applications: for embroidery, you need only a few feet. A general-purpose foot is used for straight stitching and narrow zigzag stitch; a decorative foot is needed for wider zigzag and other fancy stitches; an embroidery or darning foot is required for free-machine work; and if inserting a zip (see pp.67, 141), a zipper foot will be useful.

Needles

As with hand sewing, a variety of needles in a range of sizes is available. For general sewing use a universal needle. If stitching with decorative threads, use a machine embroidery needle, which has a larger eye for ease of threading and a slightly rounded point to prevent damage to the thread and fabric.

Fabrics

Embroidery can be worked on almost any cloth, unless you are working a counted-thread piece, in which case a fabric with an even weave is required. If you are unsure if a fabric is suitable for your project, try working a few running stitches through it; if it's easy to stitch through, it should be fine.

Fabric with an even weave (13 & 18)

These fabrics have the same number of threads per inch (tpi) in both the warp (vertical) and weft (horizontal). They are suitable for embroidery in which stitches are worked over specified numbers of threads, such as counted-thread work and most canvas work. As well as canvas, they include many different kinds of soft fabric, such as Aida (which consists of woven groups of threads) and linen with an even weave. They are graded according to fineness of weave, called the 'count', which ranges from 3.5 Aida to 32, and even finer.

Preparation

If working on a fabric with a tendency to fray, bind the edges before you start stitching. Turn over a double hem and tack (baste) it in place with pins or large stitches that can later be removed, or enclose the edges with masking tape. Fabric sealants are also available.

Threads

There is a huge array of threads for both hand and machine work, some suitable for both. The higher a thread weight, the thinner the thread. For lightweight fabrics, use a thin (high-weight) thread; for thicker fabrics, use a thicker (lower-weight) thread.

General sewing

A 40-weight thread is a popular choice for general sewing and appliqué (16). Cotton, polyester or cotton-coated polyester in a huge range of hues are available. Received wisdom is to match the thread material to that of the fabric, but this isn't necessary if you use a good-quality thread. For appliqué, use a colour that matches the motif fabric.

Tacking (basting)

Tacking thread breaks easily and doesn't stretch, so, when removed, it won't damage your work.

Hand embroidery

Threads and yarns for hand stitching are available in a massive assortment of fibres, colours, weights and finishes. Listed here are a few of the most popular. The type used will depend on what background cloth you are using, the effect you wish to create and the final use of the embroidery. But there are few hard and fast rules, so as you gain confidence, experiment with different threads and combinations to see what you think looks best.

Stranded cotton (floss; 20): This widely used durable cotton thread is suitable for stitching on most types of fabrics. It comprises six strands which are easily separated. Different results are achieved depending on how many strands are used.

Perlé: This soft cotton, non-divisible thread with a silky sheen is made of twisted strands. It is available in different weights and is suitable for a variety of embroidery projects.

Soft (matte) cotton (19): As with perlé, this thread is made of non-divisible strands, but it has a matte finish. It is ideal for canvas work, such as Bargello (see p.44).

Tapestry wool (15): This 100% wool thread is manufactured to give a smooth and even finish. It is designed for techniques like Berlin woolwork (see p.30). Finer, crewel wool is also pictured, right (14).

Decorative machine threads

A wide variety of high-gloss embroidery and metallic threads are made for machine embroidery. Other special threads are also available in a range of thicknesses and finishes.

General tips and techniques

Transferring designs

Unless you are working a counted-thread pattern or free-machine embroidery (and even then you might wish to transfer design lines) you will need to transfer embroidery templates onto the right side of your fabric. There are several ways to do this, but sometimes one method will be more suitable than another.

Tracing

Simple motifs can be traced directly on to most light-coloured cloths. First, trace the design provided on to tracing paper using either a propelling/sharp pencil or a permanent marker – the lines need to be bold enough to show through the fabric. (You may need to enlarge the original design, for example by using a photocopier, before doing

this.) With fine fabrics you might be able to see this design through the fabric when it's placed on a worktop, but it's more likely that you will need to hold both paper and fabric up to a light source – either a window or a lightbox. If using a window, tape the traced design to a window and then tape the fabric over the top. Make sure the fabric is taut and positioned correctly over the design. Trace the design on to the fabric using your chosen marker.

Dressmaker's carbon paper

For dark fabrics, dressmaker's carbon paper can be used to transfer a design. First trace the design provided on to tracing or white paper, as above. Place the dressmaker's carbon paper carbon-side down on the right side of the fabric and then place the traced design on top of it (you can hold the papers in place with pins). Then, draw over the lines of the design

with a pencil or ballpoint pen to transfer the design onto the fabric. For simple geometric designs you can use a tracing wheel (a serrated-edged wheel attached to a handle) to draw over the design.

Pressing

When your stitching is complete you might find that your work is creased or distorted. If this is the case, press the embroidery to neaten and straighten everything up before making up your project. So that you don't flatten your stitching, place the embroidery right side down on a padded pressing surface, such as a folded towel. Heat the iron to an appropriate setting; if your fabric and threads have different pressing temperatures, use whichever is the lower. Cover the work with a damp cloth; press the embroidered areas lightly and then press any unstitched background areas in the usual way. Leave the work to dry completely.

STITCH GUIDE

Refer to this guide when you come across unfamiliar stitches. It may be a good idea to practise on a piece of scrap fabric first. The illustrations assume that the stitcher is right-handed. Left-handers should reverse the direction of stitching. If your fabric is taut, you will need to work with a vertical motion and can stitch in any direction.

Running stitch

Bring the thread up through the fabric at 1, down at 2 (working right to left), up at 3, down at 4 and so on. Length of stitches and spaces can be varied for different effects. Tacking (basting) stitches are extra-long running stitches.

Backstitch

Bring the thread up through the fabric at 1 and back down at 2 (working right to left). Bring it up again at 3, then back down at 1, and so on. Aim for a continuous line of stitches with no gaps. Make shorter stitches for curved lines.

Stem stitch

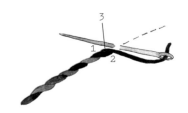

Bring the thread up through the fabric at 1 and down at 2 (working left to right). Bring it up at 3, halfway between 1 and 2, above the first stitch. Keep the thread below the needle.

Split stitch

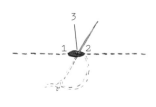

Bring the thread up through the fabric at 1 and down at 2 (working left to right). Bring it back up at 3, splitting the centre of the previous stitch.

Take the needle down at 4 and then back up through the previous stitch as before.

Feather stitch

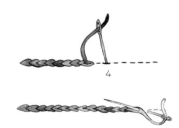

Work from top to bottom. Bring thread up through the fabric at 1 and back down at 2, leaving a loop on the front. Bring the needle back up at 3 and pull thread to shape loop, going down at 4, up again at 5, and down through 6. Work the next two stitches diagonally to the left, the following two to the right, and so on.

Satin stitch

Bring the thread up through the fabric at 1, down at 2, then back up right next to 1 and down right next to 2, filling in the required area with flat stitches that are very close together.

Padded satin stitch

Fill the required shape with satin stitches. Work another layer of satin stitches that are perpendicular to the previous row. This will create a 3D, padded effect.

Blanket/Buttonhole stitch

Take the thread down through the fabric at 1 and up at 2 (working left to right), keeping thread looped under the needle. Pull the thread through. For buttonhole stitch, work stitches closer together.

Overcast stitch

Bring the thread up through the fabric at 1, then over the edge of the fabric and up again through 2 (working from right to left). Keep stitches close together.

Whip stitch

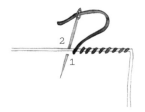

To join layered fabrics, bring the thread up through both pieces of fabric at 1 and again at 2 (working from right to left). Keep stitches small and close together.

To join abutting fabrics, bring the thread up through the bottom piece of fabric at 1. Insert into the top piece at 2, and the bottom piece at 3 (slightly to the left of your starting point). Continue to work from right to left.

Slip stitch

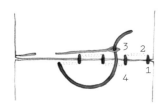

Bring the thread up through the fabric at 1 and over to 2 (working from right to left). Take it under the fabric and up at 3. Go down again at 4, and so on. Only the vertical stitches should be visible.

Chain stitch

Bring the thread up through the fabric at 1, then back down into the same hole, forming a loop. Bring up at 2, keeping looped thread behind the needle. Pull the thread to tighten loop until desired shape is achieved.

Broad/open chain stitch

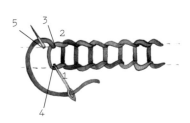

Bring the thread up through the fabric at 1, down at 2 and up at 3, looping the thread around the needle, as for chain stitch. Do not pull the thread too tight. Take the needle down again at 4, and up at 5, again making a wide loop.

Couching

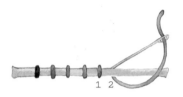

You will need two threads: a thicker (laid) thread and a thinner (couching) thread.

Place the foundation (laid) thread on the fabric, along the design line. Bring the couching thread up through the fabric at 1, under the foundation thread. Make a tiny stitch over the thread, going back into or close to 1. Bring the needle up at 2, and make another small stitch to anchor the foundation thread in place.

Tent stitch

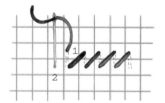

Bring the needle up through the fabric at 1 (top right) and down at 2 (bottom left), working right to left.

Underside couching

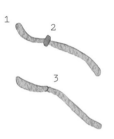

Using a large-eyed needle, bring the foundation thread up at the start of the design line (1). Bring the couching thread up through the fabric at 2, under the foundation thread. Make a tiny stitch

over the thread, going back into or close to 2. Pull on the couching thread until it disappears into the fabric (3). To finish, use a large needle to take the foundation thread to the wrong side.

Darning stitch

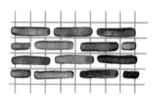

Work different-length running stitches to create the desired patterns or shapes.

Fly stitch

Bring thread up through the fabric at 1 and down at 2, leaving a loop. Come up at 3, with the needle over the loop, pulling the thread into a V-shape. Go down at 4 to anchor the V in place.

French knot

Bring the thread up through the fabric at 1. Hold thread taut with other hand and wrap once around the needle. Pull the thread to tighten and take the needle down just next to 1. Pull thread through until the knot formed sits on the surface.

Bullion knot

Work a backstitch the length of the bullion knot required. Bring the needle out again at 1, but do not pull through.

Twist the thread around the point of the needle, as many times as needed to equal the length of the backstitch.

Hold the wrapped thread and pull the needle out until the wraps lie flat on the fabric. Take the needle back through 2. Pull the thread through until the knot lies flat.

Palestrina knot

Bring the thread up through the fabric at 1. Take it down at 2 and up again at 3, then pass the needle under the stitch, without piercing the fabric. Pull the thread through.

Take the needle under the first stitch again, to the right of the previous stitch, keeping the looped thread under the needle. Pull the thread through and make a small stitch as before.

Repeat the steps to build up a line of stitches. Varying the length of the initial stitches will create different effects.

Turkey rug stitch (plush work)

Thread your needle with four strands of yarn. Bring the threads down through the fabric at 1 and back up again at 2. Pull the threads through, then down again at 3. This creates a 'holding stitch'.

Bring the needle up through the fabric, beneath the stitch, and down at 4. Do not pull tight, but leave a loop. Bring the needle up to the right of the loop, and down again through the loop at 5 to create another holding stitch. Bring the needle up at 6 and create a second loop and holding stitch as before.

Repeat the steps to complete your row, and then work further rows of stitches as required. Additional rows should be worked left to right above the previous row. On the last stitch, bring the needle up under the holding stitch and slip the needle on the underside through the back stitches to tie off before cutting the loops.

COUNTED-THREAD & CANVAS WORK

Counted-thread, or just 'counted', embroidery is a type of embroidery emphasizing regular, often repeated, patterns, created using a combination of a few, relatively simple stitches – the term normally applies to embroidery worked on fabric with an even weave, where some of the background fabric is visible, blackwork (see pp.50–59) being a prime example. In canvas work – techniques include Berlin woolwork (see pp.30–39) – stitches are worked over a canvas grid, which is normally completely covered. Both techniques are relatively simple to learn; designs are often charted, with each grid square on the chart relating to a square formed by the threads of the base fabric or a stitch worked.

Chair seat (detail), 1700–50
Linen canvas embroidered with silks, 41 x 50 cm (16⅛ x 19¾ in.)
V&A: T.178–1925

KOGIN

This Japanese form of darning-stitch embroidery (embroidery worked in parallel lines of straight stitches) originated in the Tsugaru Peninsula, in Aomori prefecture, northern Honshu, during the Edo period (1615-1868). Stitched predominantly in white thread, the technique is a form of *sashiko* stitching, but, in kogin, the parallel counted stitches are worked onto a single layer of background cloth (usually indigo-dyed), to form diamond and other geometric patterns. There are three styles of traditional kogin: *nishi* (or western), comprising diamond patterns and dense stripes over garment shoulders; *mishima* (or triple-stripe), originating in the north, with three bands dividing patterns on front and back; and *higashi* (or eastern), in which large overall designs continue from front to back without a break.

A craft born of necessity

During the harsh Tsugaru peninsula winters, farmers would try to protect themselves from the cold by wearing layers of garments made from indigo-dyed plant-based fibres (hemp and ramie are grown in the region, whereas the cotton thread used in kogin is an import). Kogin was originally used on this kind of workwear to make it stronger and more durable. By the early twentieth century, kogin had almost died out, but it has been revived for household and fashion items, and promoted as *meibutsu* (an officially recognized regional speciality).

Susan Briscoe, contemporary
facsimile of a *nanbu hishizashi*
festival apron panel (detail)
Unknown base fabric with wool
stitching, 24 x 30 cm (9½ x 11¾ in.)
Private collection

Susan Briscoe, contemporary
kogin stitching in a traditional
design (detail)
Cotton, 12 x 12 cm (4¾ x 4¾ in.)
Private collection

Kimono, 1890–1930

Women from the Tsugaru Peninsula – where this garment was made – traditionally began their training in kogin at an early age; by her wedding day, a bride was expected to have created a number of fine garments for herself and her husband. This delicate kimono features a panel worked in diamond-pattern kogin, the stitches of which have been counted onto an indigo-dyed *asa* (ramie) ground. Ramie, a plant fibre, is native to eastern Asia and has been harvested there for thousands of years, being easier to spin and weave than other plant-based fibres. Ramie in particular can be very soft, and fine ramie is considered a luxury fabric.

Plain-weave ramie with a stitched cotton design,
128 x 100 cm (50⅜ x 39⅜ in.)
V&A: FE.141–1983

BOOK COVER

A traditional kogin diamond pattern is used for this book cover, with the added interest of a darned button as a closure, and, in keeping with historical precedent, the palette is white on a blue ground (though any contrasting pair of colours can be used). Great for a gift or for protecting your favourite book when you commute!

You will need

Navy blue 14-count Aida: the finished project shown here required cloth at 40 x 25 cm (16 x 10 in.) to cover a book measuring approx. 9 x 14 cm (3½ x 5½ in.), plus an extra 5 x 5 cm (2 x 2 in.) piece for the button cover

White ribbon, 3 mm (⅛ in.) wide, 50 cm (20 in.)

Self-cover button, 28 mm (1⅛ in.)

2 skeins stranded cotton (floss), white

General sewing thread in contrasting colour

General sewing thread to match Aida

Tapestry needle, size 24

Hand-sewing needle

Embroidery, or other sharp, fine-pointed scissors

Fabric scissors

Pins

Optional

Coloured pencil, for marking chart

Project by Lucy Barter

How to make

Do not pull your stitches too tight – you may distort the fabric and the cover will not fit.

1 Using the grid of the Aida as a guide, and following the template on p.28 and the chart on p.29, mark out the area of your book cover and the main stitching area using pins. Tack (baste) a **running stitch** (see p.14) in place of the pins to act as a guide, using a contrasting thread.

2 Cut a forearm-length piece of stranded cotton thread. The thread consists of six strands; separate each of them before threading them all into the tapestry needle and tie a small, tight knot in the end.

3 The stitching will be done by counting using the chart provided (see p.29). Each square on the chart represents one hole in the Aida fabric. Start the design at one end of the grid, stitch the entire bottom row and then work up, stitching each row in turn; if you find it easier, you can stitch each triangle separately. Bring the thread up from the back of the fabric on the side you plan to stitch. Right-handers will be more comfortable working from right to left, and left-handers the opposite. Stitches should lie flat on the fabric. Take care not to pull your stitches too tight, to avoid distorting your fabric.

4 Refer to the grid for each stitch. Count the holes and bring the needle up and then down according to the length of the stitch shown. **Tip:** *To keep track of your progress, use a coloured pencil to mark each stitch on the grid as you go along.* To finish a thread, take it to the back of the work and weave through a few of the stitches, then snip away the tail. Starting a new thread can be done in the same way, by weaving through existing stitches on the back.

5 On a separate piece of fabric, stitch the pattern for the button in the same way. You will use this to cover a metal button.

6 Once all the stitching is complete, you are ready to make up the book cover. Start by cutting the Aida back to leave the 1 cm (⅜ in.) allowance along the top and bottom of the book outline. Do not trim down the sides yet.

7 Place the embroidery face down and fold the allowance of fabric over along the tacking line. Press flat with your fingers. With your hand-sewing needle and matching thread, stitch a running stitch along the fold, on the fabric grain, about two or three holes from the edge, to form a 'hem'. This should not overlap the embroidery.

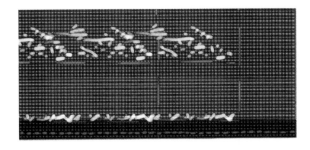

8 Cut back the short edges of the Aida, leaving a 1 cm (⅜ in.) 'hem' allowance. Repeat the hemming process at each end, making sure the corners stay square.

9 Cut out the button pattern, leaving at least a 5 mm (³⁄₁₆ in.) allowance around it. Place this over the dome part of the metal cover button and push the back in, making sure that all the fabric is tucked in.

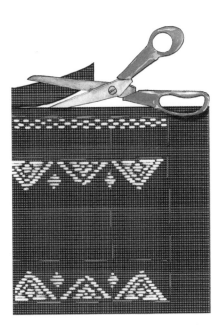

Stitch the button cover on a separate piece of matching navy Aida, before cutting out.

10 Stitch one end of the ribbon to the front cover, just to the right of where the button will be attached (indicated by a dot on the template). Then stitch the button in place with the sewing thread, right next to where the cord has been attached.

11 Fold in the front flap of the book cover along the tacking line and pin in place, keeping all corners square. Using the matching sewing thread, **whip stitch** (see p.15) the two folds of fabric together.

12 Repeat the process for the back flap of the book and remove all tacking stitches.

13 Add a knot at the end of the ribbon and wrap around the book and then the button to close the book.

Now try...

Using Aida (a very versatile fabric), in combination with darning patterns, to create a variety of effects. You can use different colours to create shading through the stitching pattern, or even use fine silk ribbons for texture. Alternatively, apply the same patterns to clothing, bags or household linens with an even weave. To make a cover for a larger book, repeat the pattern to fill the required area, taking into account the required positioning of complete triangle shapes.

Template

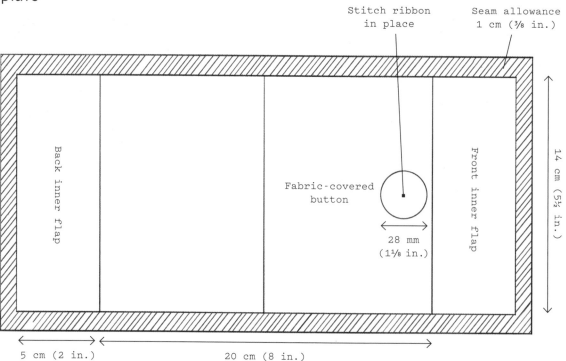

Stitch ribbon in place

Seam allowance 1 cm (³⁄₈ in.)

Back inner flap

Fabric-covered button

Front inner flap

28 mm (1¹⁄₈ in.)

14 cm (5½ in.)

5 cm (2 in.)

20 cm (8 in.)

Chart

Seam allowance
1 cm (⅜ in.)

Button

Top

Bottom

BERLIN WOOLWORK

A hard-wearing embroidery stitched through canvas fabric, Berlin woolwork was a creation of the nineteenth century. A characteristic of this type of embroidery is the use of patterns printed on 'point' paper, with squares corresponding to the squares on the canvas. Produced in Berlin, these were known as Berlin patterns. First published in the early 1800s, they were printed in black and white and the squares then hand-coloured. As they were mostly available on single sheets, they were affordable and started to sell in large numbers; the craze for Berlin woolwork began.

An international trend

By the 1830s, these patterns were also popular outside Germany; in England, they were sold by firms such as Wilks of Regent Street, London; more than 14,000 different patterns had been imported into the country by 1840. Favourite designs were stylized floral bouquets and wreaths, and scenes based on Victorian paintings. Traditionally, many bold shades of wool (progress in dyeing techniques had made a wide range of brightly coloured yarns commercially available) were used to create three-dimensional effects. Usually, a design was worked in just a single stitch, such as tent stitch. As the embroidery completely covers the canvas on which it is worked, it is strong and durable – perfect for furniture coverings and cushions for the Victorian home. By the late 1800s, however, changing tastes saw Berlin woolwork replaced by less flamboyant styles such as Art Needlework (see p.96).

Hertz and Wegener, design for Berlin woolwork, c.1860
Lithograph coloured by hand,
20.5 x 20.5 cm (8⅛ x 8⅛ in.)
V&A: E.3727-1915

Design for Berlin woolwork, 1825-50
Etching coloured by hand
V&A: E.1489-1959

Design for Berlin woolwork, 19th century

This hand-painted embroidery design (or 'Berlin pattern') for Berlin woolwork was executed entirely in watercolour and ink. We know very little about the pattern maker/publisher beyond the name printed on the design – 'A. Todt' – though a handful of such names (Carl F.W. Wicht, Herz and Wegener, G.E. Falbe), appear repeatedly on the many examples surviving from the period. The bright design of white-and-yellow convolvulus on a red background seems to have been intended as a border, perhaps for an item of clothing or as part of a broader decorative design. Worked on canvas, the finished embroidery would have been robust enough for use on home furnishings – the design may have been intended for a bellpull or similar.

Watercolour and ink, 19.5 x 32.2 cm (7⅝ x 12⅝ in.)
V&A: E.2034–1935

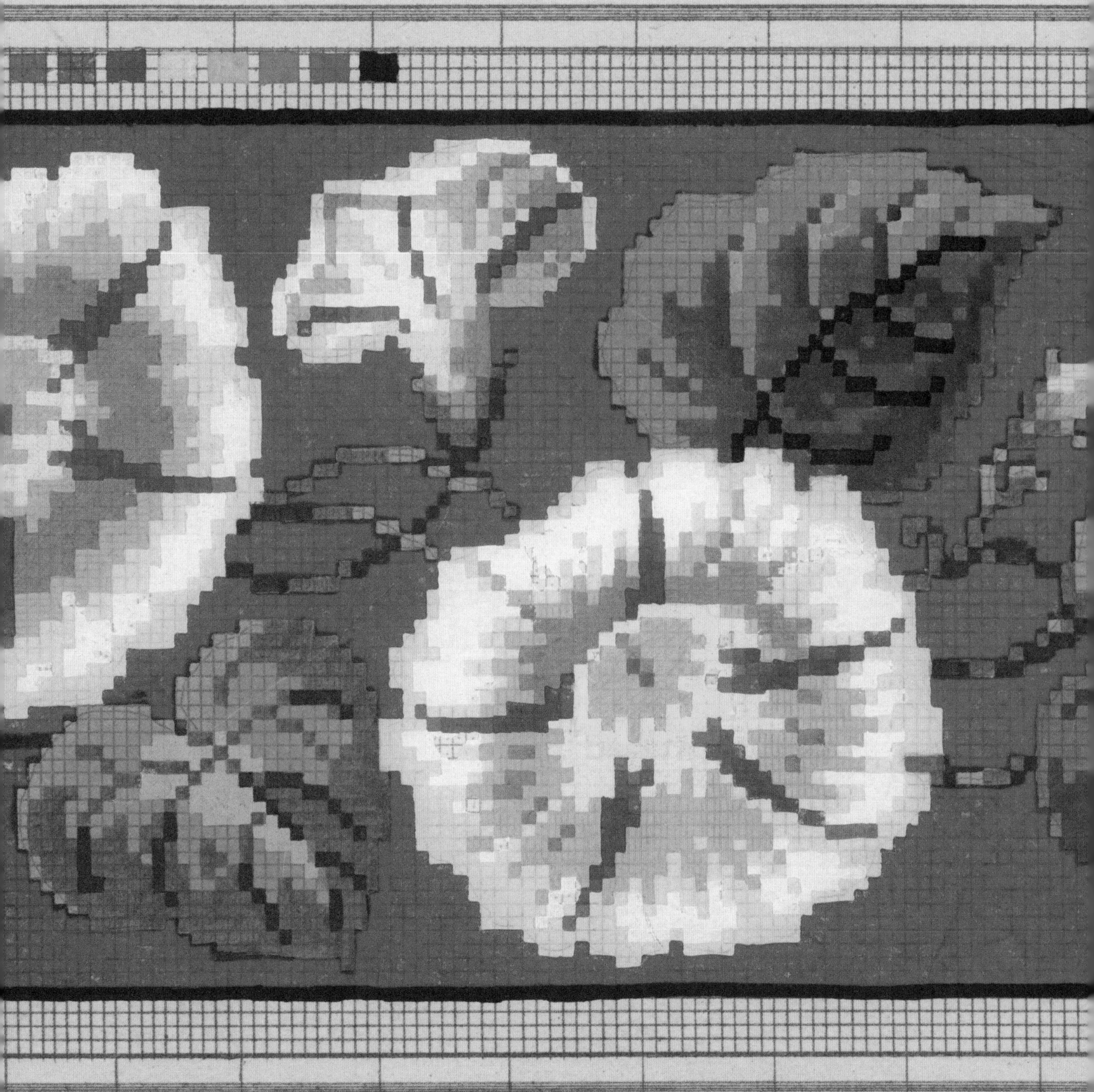

HEADBAND

This project – inspired by a nineteenth-century hand-painted design for woolwork (see pp.32–33) – is colourful and fun to stitch. Tent stitch is used to create shading, and the addition of plush work, turkey rug stitch and beads creates texture.

You will need

14 tpi mono/single-thread canvas (see p.12), 48 x 10 cm (18 x 4 in.)

Red cotton lining fabric, 50 x 12 cm (19 ½ x 4 ¾ in.)

Red ribbon (2 cm/¾ in. wide), 60 cm (24 in.)

Tapestry wool, Appletons: two skeins 504 (red), one skein 426 (light green), one skein 430 (medium green), one skein 438 (dark green), one skein 997 (light yellow), one skein 844 (dark yellow), one skein 991B (white), one skein 875 (light grey), one skein 963 (dark grey)

General sewing thread, to match lining fabric

General sewing thread, to match bead colour

Dark green seed beads, size 11

Tapestry needle, size 20

Beading needle, size 10

Embroidery, or other sharp, fine-pointed scissors

Masking tape

Fabric scissors

Pins

For blocking (if needed)

Wooden board, 2 cm (¾ in.) thick

Sheet of plastic, to cover the wood

Water in a spray bottle

Nails

Small hammer

Optional

Rectangular embroidery frame

Tissue paper

Project by Lucy Barter

How to make

1 Prepare the canvas by cutting away any selvedge and taping the edges with masking tape – half over the edge of the canvas and half folded to the back – to prevent fraying.

2 Tack (baste) a line around the area to be stitched, using the sewing thread and tapestry needle. Mark, with tacking, the centre of the area to be stitched, horizontally and vertically, referring to the chart on p.39. This helps you to centre the design and will act as a guide for stitching.

3 Berlin woolwork is best stitched in a frame. This helps to keep the horizontal and vertical grain of the canvas straight. Use stretcher bars that fit the project and pin the canvas to the bars. Since this work is narrow, this project could also be worked very successfully in hand.

4 Cut a forearm-length strand of white tapestry wool, thread into the tapestry needle and knot the end. Start with the thread on top of the canvas, a short distance away from where you will start stitching. As you stitch back toward the knot, the thread will be covered on the back and secure enough in the end to cut the knot away. Begin by filling in all of the **tent stitch** (see below and p.16).

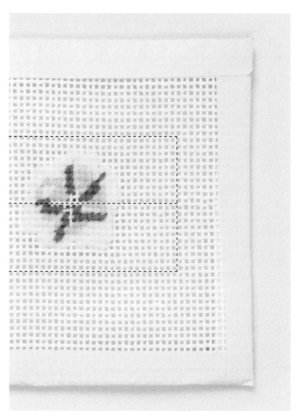

Tape the edges of the canvas and tack (baste) guidelines in place before you start stitching.

Stitch diagram

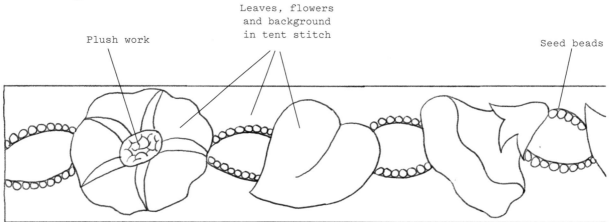

Plush work

Leaves, flowers and background in tent stitch

Seed beads

5 Using the diagram below and the chart on p.39, start the tent stitch in the first motif of the design. Work through the colours of each motif in turn. Each colour in the embroidery has been indicated by a different symbol on the chart. Fill in all the tent stitch areas first, leaving the plush work and beading until later.

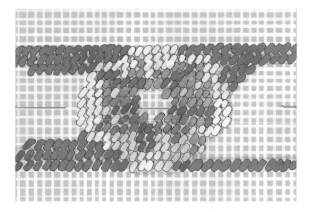

6 Using the beading needle and hand-sewing thread, double the thread in the needle and stitch the beads in place as indicated on the chart.

7 Plush work is done last, using **turkey rug stitch** (see p.17). When complete, cut back the threads, leaving fibres standing up over the work. **Tip:** *Before cutting, cover the embroidery with tissue paper, with holes cut where the plush work is. This will prevent the cut fibres from getting everywhere. You can also use masking tape to pick up loose fibres.*

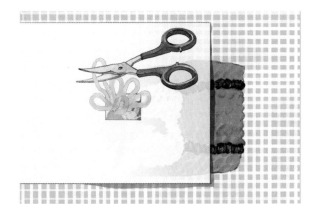

Leave any plush work until all other stitches have been worked.

8 Remove your finished embroidery from the frame, if using, and remove the tacking. The work may need to be blocked to stretch it back into shape if distorted. If so, cover the wooden board with the plastic and lay the canvas on top, face up. Spray the work with a fine mist of water until just damp (do not drench the canvas).

9 Place a nail in the centre of the top of the canvas, a few threads in from the edge. Hammer the nail in slightly, just enough to hold the canvas in place. Repeat at the bottom of the design, making sure the embroidery is square. Do the same at the sides of the work and then add nails, 8-10 threads apart, gently pulling the canvas each time so it is straight. You will need to keep spraying the work so it does not dry out during this process. Leave to dry and then remove all nails.

10 To finish, cut away the excess canvas to 1 cm (⅜ in.) from the design edge. Cut away each of the corners at an angle to reduce bulk when the canvas is folded back. Fold the ends of the canvas back tightly and finger-press, then, using a double length of sewing thread (for strength) **whip stitch** (see p.15) the edge of the canvas to the stitches on the back. Repeat at the top and bottom of the design.

11 Cut the ribbon in half to form two ties, and stitch one end of each to each end of the canvas, leaving the tails of the ribbon free. So that the ends of the ribbon do not fray, fold over by 5 mm (⅛ in.) once, then twice, and sew down.

12 Fold back the edges of the lining fabric by 1 cm (⅜ in.) to match the canvas and press the folds. Pin to the back of the canvas, wrong sides together, and **whip stitch** (see p.15) the edges, making sure the free end of the ribbon does not get caught up in the lining.

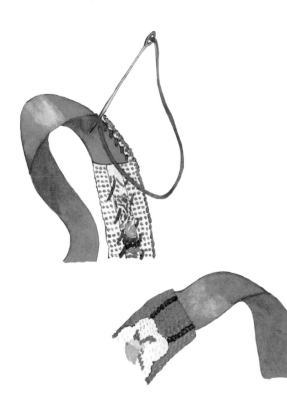

Now try...

Making larger or smaller versions of the project. The chart can simply be repeated on a longer canvas to create longer accessories, like a belt or a camera strap. Design details from the chart can also be reduced in size and stitched on a smaller-count canvas to create jewellery inserts for rings, lockets and brooches.

Chart

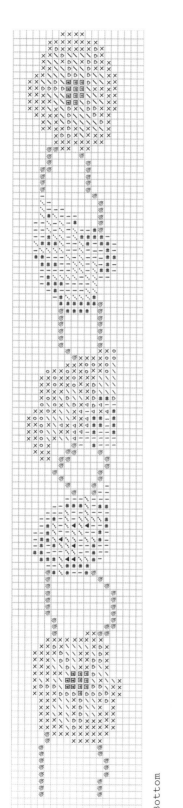

Top

Bottom

Thread key

Symbol	Thread
✕	White (991B)
╱	Light grey (875)
◯	Dark grey (963)
♡	Red (504)
│	Light green (426)
♯	Medium green (430)
⸭	Dark green (438)
▲	Dark yellow (844)
◪	Dark yellow (844) plush
△	Light yellow (997)
◬	Light yellow (997) plush
▨	Bead

To stitch a longer design, repeat the
pattern by lining up the stems of the
end of the design to the edge of the white
flower. You could also cluster two or more
flowers together, by following the chart.

BARGELLO

Usually stitched on single-thread canvas, bargello, named for the Bargello Palace in Florence, is characterized by the use of just one stitch, the Florentine stitch. In the simplest, classic row (band) design, each stitch is worked vertically over four threads of canvas, with adjacent stitches jumping either two up or two down to form regular peaks and valleys. Once set, the pattern is repeated in subsequent rows until stitching completely covers the canvas. Variations on this basic four/two pattern give rise to countless wave-like designs. The use of colour to define the pattern is also characteristic of bargello, with adjacent rows worked in different tones or tints to create glorious effects.

Disputed origins

The origins of bargello are uncertain, as indicated by the variety of names it is given: flame stitch, Florentine work, Hungarian point and Irish stitch. It has been suggested that a Hungarian bride marrying into the wealthy Medici family took the work with her to Italy in the fifteenth century. Whatever its origins, this form of work was abundant and highly developed in Florence during the Italian Renaissance and was traditionally used to make domestic upholstery. The use of vibrant shades can produce bold and exciting results. Designs have also evolved to produce mirror-image patterns that form diamonds or curved motifs, and four-way patterns that produce even more complex compositions.

Shoes, c.1730-50
Embroidered linen canvas
V&A: T.64&A-1935

Chair seat, 1700-50
Linen canvas embroidered with
silks, 41 x 50 cm (16¼ x 19¾ in.)
V&A: T.178-1925

Pincushion, 1670–80

This small example of bargello – among the many variant names given to this style of embroidery, 'flame stitch' most accurately describes the jagged, flame-like patterns seen here – is known to have been worked by a young English girl called Martha Edlin (1660–1725). Her many embroideries, worked from the age of eight onwards, were cherished and passed down by her female descendants over 300 years; this particular example is in perfect condition, seemingly never having been used for its intended purpose. An elaborate casket, with embroidered panels worked by Edlin (see opposite), is also held in the V&A collections.

Silk embroidered with silk, 6.3 x 7.5 cm (2½ x 3 in.)
V&A: T.446–1990

Assorted embroidered
items by Martha
Edlin, 1670-80

ZIPPED POUCH

This little pouch or purse – perfect for make-up or just your keys and coins – is embellished with a simple wave design, worked in bargello embroidery using horizontal bands of bright, bold colour. Once you've mastered the basic technique, you can experiment with different colour palettes, and customize the finished object!

You will need

White or tan single-thread (mono) canvas, 18 tpi, 50 x 30 cm (20 x 12 in.)

Lining fabric in a complementary colour, 28 x 18 cm (11 x 7 in.)

15 cm (6 in.) zip, in a complementary colour

Short length of ribbon or leather, for zip pull

DMC Soft Cotton thread: one skein 2907 (light green), one skein 2905 (mid green), one skein 2890 (dark green), one skein 2172 (dark grey), one skein 2820 (dark blue), one skein 2797 (mid blue), one skein 2826 (light blue), one skein 2233 (light grey), one skein 2726 (yellow), one skein 2741 (orange), one skein 2349 (bright red)

General sewing thread, to match zip

Hand-sewing needle

Tapestry needle, size 22

Sewing machine, with zipper foot

Pins

Project by Rachel Doyle

How to make

Start with light green, and follow the chart for subsequent colours.

1 The completed embroidery will measure approx. 35.5 by 16 cm (14 x 6¼ in.). Centre your design on the canvas.

2 The first row of the bargello pattern is worked in light green and starts in the top-left corner of the design. Thread a single strand of the cotton in your tapestry needle and knot the end. Take your needle down through the top of the work, approx. 3 cm (1 in.) ahead of your starting point, within the body of the design, so as to enclose the end in the stitches.

3 Following the chart on p.49, work the top row of the wave design in the first colour, as shown above. Each stitch is always across four threads of the canvas (or five holes). Stitch each row from left to right. To end the thread, weave the needle through the stitches on the reverse and trim the excess.

4 Work the next row in mid green, ending each stitch in the same hole that the first light-green stitch ends in. Stitch the next nine rows, changing colour as directed.

5 After the final row, start again with the light green and work through all the colours again. Stitch a further two repeats, so that the entire pattern is sewn four times.

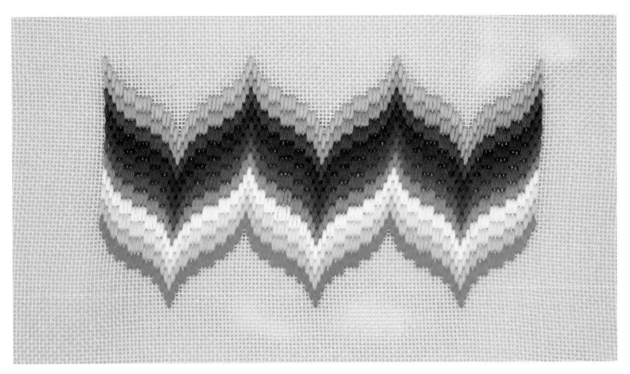

Work through all eleven colours in the sequence shown, before filling in the top and bottom edges.

6 At the beginning and end of the design, you will have 'v'-shaped gaps. Fill these in, continuing the colour sequence. Shorten the stitches at the beginning and end of each colour so that they finish on a straight line (see finishing chart below).

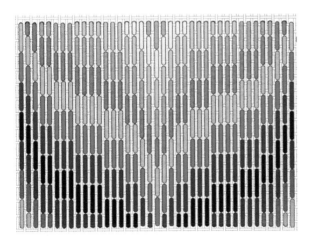

7 Once the embroidery is complete, block if necessary (see p.38, steps 8-9) and trim the canvas, leaving approx. 1 cm (⅜ in.) around the design.

8 Pin one half of the zip to the top edge of the right side of the canvas, with the zipper facing down. Using a zipper foot, stitch the zip to the canvas, along the top edge only, sewing as close to the bargello stitching as possible.

9 Pin the second, unsewn side of the zip to the other end of the canvas, making sure the two sides of the embroidery line up. Stitch together in the same way.

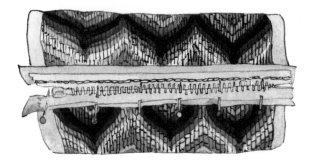

10 Pin the sides of the purse together, wrong sides facing. Make sure the edges of the bargello line up exactly. Open the zip. Again using a zipper foot, machine-stitch the two side edges. Turn the whole right side out to check your stitching; if there is any canvas still showing at the edges, stitch again a little closer in.

Now try...

Making the final bargello piece to a larger size, simply by increasing the number of design repeats. It could become a cushion or an applied pocket on a canvas bag. You can also design your own stitch patterns, using graph paper and the guidelines set out here and on p.58.

11 Fold your lining fabric in half, right sides together, and stitch a 1 cm (⅜ in.) seam down both short sides. You may want to turn your bargello pouch right side out at this point, slip the lining into it and check the fit. If the lining is too small, you will need to unpick one or both seams, and re-stitch.

12 Fold back 1 cm (⅜ in.) around the open edge, press and then turn the lining through.

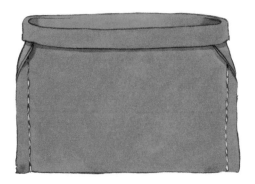

13 With the bargello pouch inside out, slip the lining over it and align the edge with the seam joining zip and canvas. Pin the two together. **Slip stitch** (see p.15) the lining to the zip.

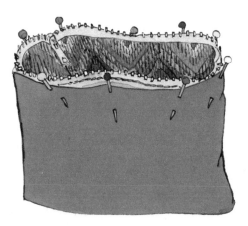

14 Turn the whole pouch right side out and attach a leather or ribbon pull to the zip by tying it firmly in place.

Chart

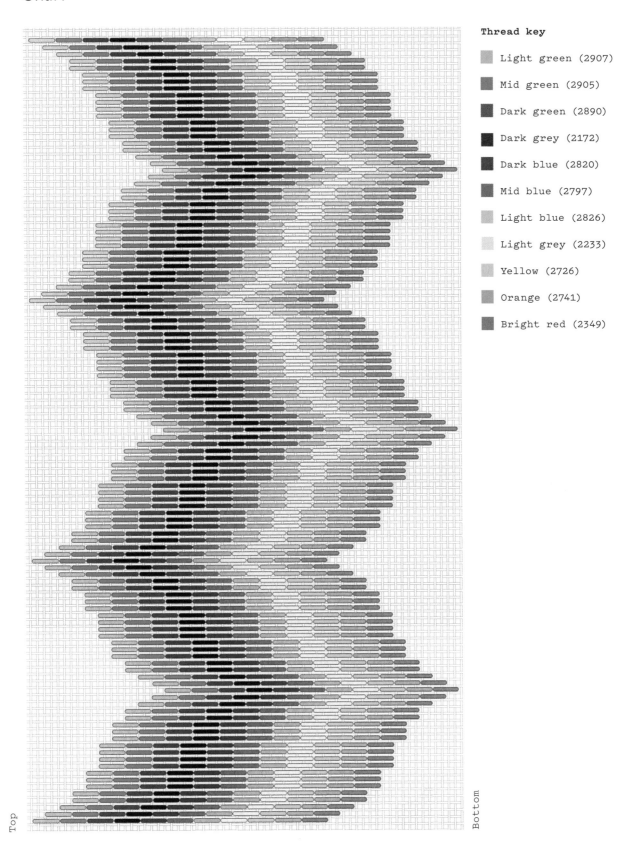

Thread key

- Light green (2907)
- Mid green (2905)
- Dark green (2890)
- Dark grey (2172)
- Dark blue (2820)
- Mid blue (2797)
- Light blue (2826)
- Light grey (2233)
- Yellow (2726)
- Orange (2741)
- Bright red (2349)

Top

Bottom

BLACKWORK

This elegant, monochromatic style of embroidery has romantically been referred to as 'Spanish work', based on the belief that Catherine of Aragon made the technique popular in England when she brought it with her from Spain in 1501. But it was known in England long before then and is mentioned as decoration for a white smock in Chaucer's late-fourteenth-century narrative poem *The Canterbury Tales*. Originally worked in black silk on a natural white linen background, designs were sometimes embellished with metallic threads. Traditionally, blackwork was used as a decoration on costume accessories such as caps, collars, cuffs and sleeves, a fashion that was widespread throughout Europe in the sixteenth and seventeenth centuries.

Evolving designs

Usually worked on fabric with an even weave, sixteenth-century blackwork used counted stitches to form small repeating geometric or floral shapes; the all-over filling patterns were called 'diaper' fillings. By the early seventeenth century, larger, more naturalistic designs had appeared. Sinuous stems connecting flowers and leaves, interspersed with birds, animals and insects, were particularly popular (see overleaf). These designs could be printed or otherwise transferred directly onto the linen, but professional embroiderers or artists were also hired to draw new patterns freehand. Inspired by woodcuts and engravings, designs might be further enhanced by 'speckling'. This technique creates the effect of shading through the use of tiny running stitches. Modern blackwork is generally a counted-thread technique, with the success of the design dependent on the choice and placement of stitches to create different tonal effects.

Smock (part, with reconstructed skirt), 1575-85
Embroidered linen, 116 x 61 cm
(45⅝ x 24 in.; across arms)
V&A: T.113 to 118-1997

Sleeve panel, 1610–20

The insects in the step-by-step project overleaf were directly inspired by two pieces of seventeenth-century blackwork – both embroidered in silk thread on linen – held in the collections of the V&A. The dragonfly originates in this sleeve panel, which originally formed part of a woman's jacket; it is accompanied by other insects, including beetles, moths and caterpillars, and a single, delicate spider's web enlivens the whole design. Worked in the 'speckling' style, this panel features tiny running stitches, which mimic the subtle shading seen in contemporary woodblock prints.

Linen sleeve embroidered with silk thread, 61.5 x 21.5 cm
(24¼ x 8½ in.)
V&A: T.11–1950 (mounted with a nightcap panel, right)

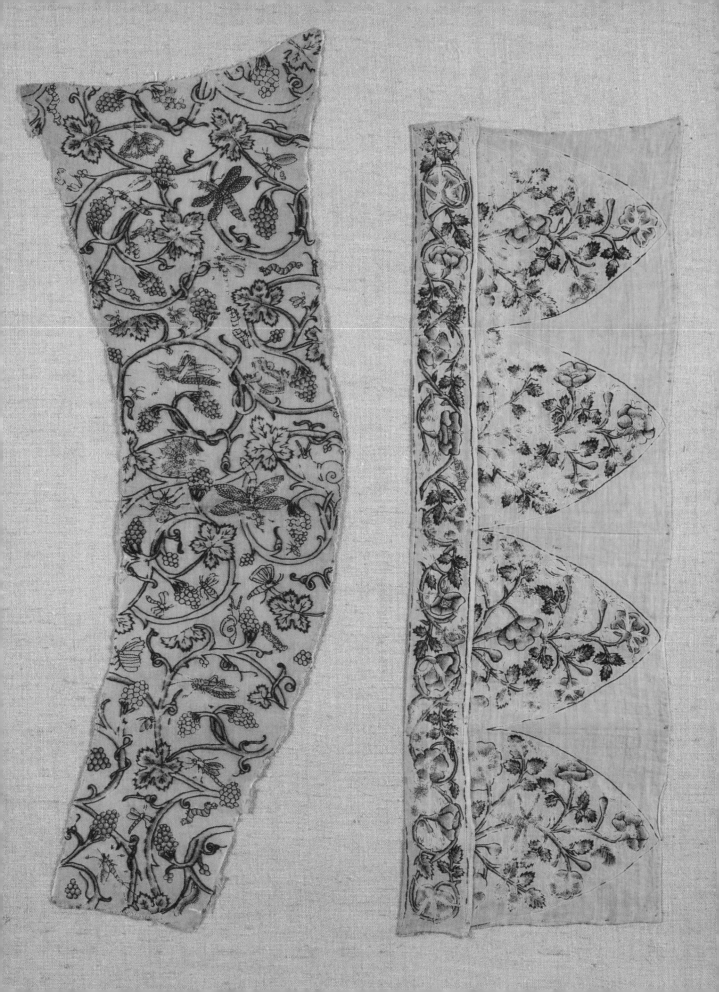

INSECT NAPKINS

The geometric stitch patterns of blackwork embroidery are known as diaper patterns. Specially designed for these insect-themed napkins, the patterns shown here were inspired by moth and dragonfly motifs in Stuart textiles held by the V&A (see pp.52–53) – early examples of the technique as practised in England.

You will need

22-count Hardanger fabric; size will depend on desired size of napkins (see p.56)
1 skein DMC perlé cotton thread, size 12, 310 (black)
1 skein stranded cotton (floss), black
General sewing thread, white
Tapestry needle, size 24
Sharps needle, size 9
Fabric scissors
Pins
Embroidery, or other sharp, fine-pointed scissors
Black waterproof pen

Optional

13 cm (5 in.) embroidery hoop

Project by Sarah Homfray

How to make

1 First, cut and hem your napkins. Cut your fabric to the required size (traditional sizes are 41 x 46 cm/ 16 x 18 in. for a rectangle, or 41 cm/ 16 in. square), adding on 2 cm (¾ in.) for the hem allowance.

2 Measure 2 cm (¾ in.) along one side from the corner of your fabric, and then 2 cm from the same corner along the other side. Mark these points and cut off the corner. Repeat for the other three corners. Fold the flattened-off corners 1.5 cm (⅝ in.) towards the middle of the napkin, and then 1 cm (⅜ in.) along each long side, following the grain of the fabric, and press. Fold each side in again by another 1 cm (⅜ in.). Your corners should meet to create a mitre. Press all folds and corners flat. Pin in place, ready for hemming.

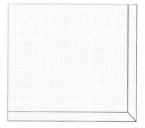

3 Using a single strand of the white sewing thread and the sharps needle, hem all of the edges using **whip stitch** (see p.15).

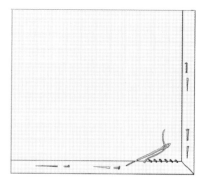

4 Wash the napkin in warm soapy water at this stage. Allow to dry and iron flat.

5 If you like, you can secure your fabric in an embroidery hoop to stitch the moth pattern, though it is not necessary.

Moth

1 The moth design (see p.59) can be embroidered straight onto the fabric, by counting the design onto the fabric as you go (follow the order laid out in steps 2–7). Work in **backstitch** (see p.14), following the chart: each square equals one square of your fabric; the black lines are the stitching. Don't work over more than two threads of the fabric at once. Measure 5 cm (2 in.) from the bottom right corner of your napkin and mark with a pin – this will be where the point of the moth's tail sits.

2 Thread your needle with the perlé cotton thread and knot the end. Take your thread down through the fabric in the middle of where the body will be stitched, bring the thread up at the tip of the tail and work back towards the knot so that the stitches cover the loose thread on the back of the embroidery, securing it; when you have finished, you can cut away the knot. To finish your stitches at any stage, turn the work over and thread the needle a couple of times through stitches you have just worked, then cut the thread off.

Work the outlines first and then fill in with the diaper patterns.

3 Start at the tip of the tail and work around the individual main body sections. Fill in the middle of each section before moving on to the next. Work around the head and add the antennae. The moth is symmetrical so you will need to count carefully!

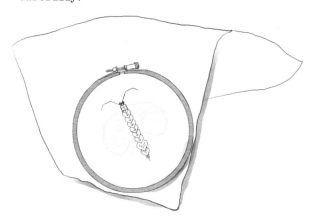

4 Now work the outline of each main wing shape, ensuring they are symmetrical. **Tip:** *Note where the wings join the body to help you with this!*

5 Finally work the outlines of the two lower wings.

6 Once the outline of the design is in place, you can work the diaper fillings. Cut a forearm-length piece of the stranded cotton and separate one strand for working the stitches. Start with the lower wings and work your way up and down the pattern, filling in the wing shapes.

7 Now work the main wings, starting at the top of one wing, near the body. Note that the pattern is broken up at the edge to leave a white space all the way around the wing. This pattern is a bit more complicated than the body and wing outlines, so count the stitches carefully and note where they meet in relation to the body to help you! **Tip:** *If you find counting the edges of the pattern a bit difficult, you could just fill in the whole of the wing shape instead.*

Dragonfly

This design is slightly different from that of the moth in that the fillings are counted patterns but the outlines are stitched freestyle rather than counted.

1 Trace the design template (below) on to your napkin with a waterproof black pen (see p.13 for full instructions).

2 Starting with the main body this time, work the pattern inside your outline shape using one strand of stranded cotton. Work the upper wing patterns at this stage also.

3 Work a **stem stitch** (see p.14) around the body and upper wing shapes using the perlé cotton thread.

4 Work a stem stitch around the lower wing shapes, then fill in the pattern in the middle of these wings. Note that the lower wings overlap the upper wings, and the pattern is fragmented in places, for a lacy effect.

5 Work the pattern inside the tail using one strand of stranded cotton – creating 'shading', as shown, or as you prefer – then stem stitch around each tail section.

6 Work the antennae in stem stitch, then work the small diaper pattern for the eyes to complete your dragonfly.

Trim off all loose threads neatly when your stitching is complete.

Template

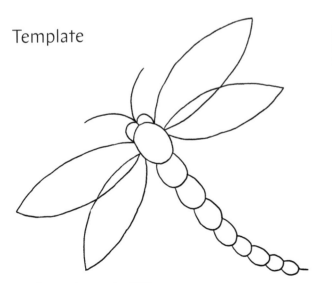

Template shown at 100%

Now try...

Plotting your own insects! Many museum collections include blackwork designs, but you don't have to be limited to these; you can find inspiration in photographs, textile designs and illustrations. A counted design is stitched by following the holes in the fabric, so trace an original design onto graph paper, using pencil, then go over the drawing using pen, following the grid lines, to make the shape conform to the fabric weave.

Charts

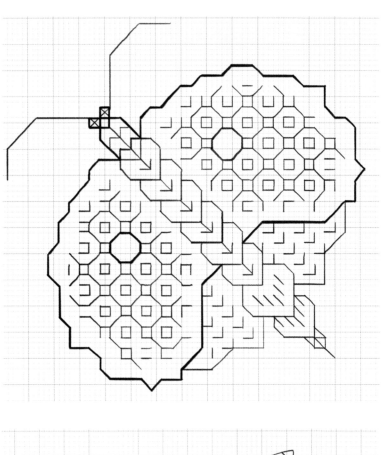

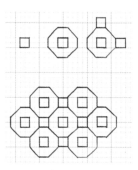

Upper wing pattern –
start with a square
and work hexagons
around each square.

Lower wing
pattern

Body pattern

Eye pattern

Lower wing
pattern

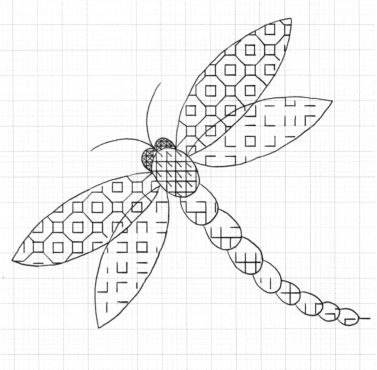

PHULKARI

The Panjab region, comprising areas of North India and eastern Pakistan, is famous for its *phulkari* ('flower work'). Traditionally, designs were embroidered from the reverse, using darning stitches counted over the threads of a cotton background cloth (called *khaddar*). Handwoven locally, *khaddar* used for *phulkari* was often dyed in shades of red. The stitching is worked in vibrantly coloured silk floss, the colours frequently including gold, yellow, white, orange and red. Light reflected off the groups of stitches, worked in vertical, horizontal and diagonal directions, creates glowing, textured effects. Modern *phulkari* motifs can be counted over fabric with an even weave, or the motifs can be drawn onto the background instead; the stitching can be worked from the back or the front. Contemporary designers have embraced the technique, incorporating *phulkari* into clothing, as well as home accessories.

A historical craft revived

Phulkari originally referred to the embroidered headcovers and garments that were traditionally part of rural Panjabi women's everyday dress. A domestic craft, passed down through generations, *phulkari* were made by women for themselves and family members; designs varied from figurative to wholly geometric. Special *phulkari* headcovers called *bagh* (garden; see overleaf) were made for weddings and ceremonial occasions. The ground of these shawls was fully, or nearly fully, covered in embroidery in striking geometric patterns. After the division of the Panjab between India and Pakistan in 1947, *phulkari* work virtually died out. But the skills have now been revived, and in 2011 'geographical indication' (GI) status was awarded to the *phulkari* technique to help preserve its link to the Panjab.

Headcover/shawl, early 20th century
Cotton embroidered with silk floss,
222 x 146 cm (87⅜ x 57½ in.)
V&A: IS.24-1983

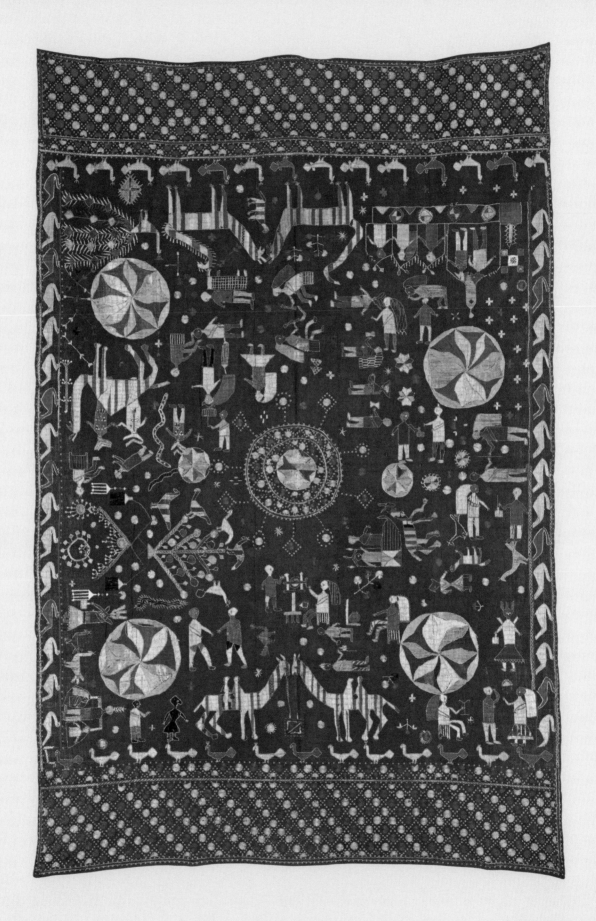

Shawl, 19th century

This vibrant shawl – from the Panjab region – is made of hand-spun cotton, embroidered with surface darning stitch in a lozenge pattern, using a restrained palette of silk threads. This kind of *phulkari* shawl is known as *bagh*, meaning 'garden': the bold, regular, geometric design created by the embellishment covers and conceals the cotton ground entirely. It is softened somewhat by the subtle modulation of yellow tones in the embroidery.

Cotton embroidered with silk floss, 241 x 129 cm (93 x 50 in.)
V&A: IS.3–1961

TASSELLED CUSHION

This cushion features a panel of embroidery, made using colours and design elements from the nineteenth-century shawl shown on p.63. A section of the shawl's border design is used along one edge, and the main design is placed deliberately off-centre, as though it were a fragment of an older textile, being re-used. You can arrange the colours as you wish. The instructions include options for a zip at the centre-back of the cushion, or for simply stitching it closed.

You will need

Deep orange 25-count Lugana (or other fabric with an even weave), min. 34 x 34 cm (13½ x 13½ in.). **Note:** *The colour counts here, as you'll be able to see it between your stitches!*

Silk or artificial silk fabric (matching or complementing one of the colours in the embroidery), 75 cm (29½ in.) x width of fabric (WOF)

8 x 11 cm (4¼ in.) tassels (or four larger tassels), to complement embroidery colours

Cushion pad (pillow form), 46 cm (18 in.) square

DMC stranded cotton (floss): four skeins 3866 (ivory), four skeins 783 (gold), one skein 3804 (hot pink), one skein 727 (pale yellow), one skein 742 (orange), one skein 3799 (charcoal grey), one skein 166 (lime green)

General sewing thread, to match the fabric

Tacking (basting) thread

Embroidery needle, size 7

Tape measure

Fabric scissors

Sewing machine

Zipper foot (you will need this even if you are not using a zip)

Optional

Embroidery hoop or rectangular embroidery frame

40 cm (16 in.) zip, to match the fabric

Project by Caroline Crabtree

How to make

1 First, you will need to make a few design decisions. Do you want to include the zigzag border design? (You could omit it, and work the main design across the whole area.) Do you prefer the design to be symmetrical, with a clear centre point?

2 Measure out a 30 cm (11¾ in.) square on your even-weave fabric, leaving at least a 2 cm (¾ in.) border around the square as your seam allowance. Cut out this larger area. **Tip:** *The fabric will fray with handling, so overcast, or machine stitch around the edges using zigzag.*

3 Tack (baste) around the edge of the 30 cm (11¾ in.) square, so that it is marked out in the centre of the fabric.

4 If you are working the border design, count 48 threads in from one side of the square, and tack a line parallel to this side, as shown below. If you are not working the border, and want the main design to be centred, tack two centre lines – 15 cm (6 in.) from the edge, both vertically and horizontally.

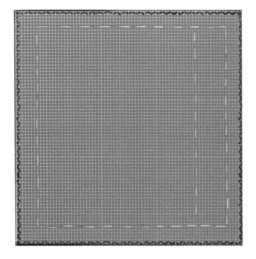

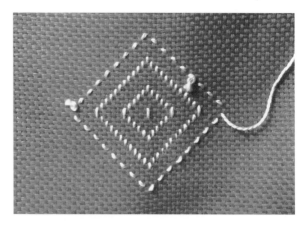

Very little stitching appears on the reverse of the main design.

5 For all of the embroidery, use three of the six strands of embroidery cotton. Separate each strand individually, then recombine them and thread your needle; this will give a fuller, smoother finish to the stitching.

6 Start by stitching the border (if you are including it) in the area that you have marked out, following the stitching charts provided (p.69) and the colours shown in the photograph (p.65). This part of the design is worked in counted surface satin stitch, which gives a slightly firmer fabric than the main part of the design. All stitches are vertical and take the embroidery thread over four threads of the fabric. Take the stitching up to the tacked edges of your square. You will see that almost all stitching shows on the surface, with very little on the reverse.

7 The main body of the design is made up of stitched squares, arranged into diamonds (see chart on p.69). If you are using the border design, you can begin the main design at any point, and repeat it to fill the space. If you want the main design to be centred, count 52 threads from the centre, and begin the first square.

8 Work the squares of the main design. Note that each stitch has one thread between it and the next, so that the colour of the base fabric is seen through the embroidery. All of the stitches are vertical and most cross five threads. First, work the large diamonds (five squares wide on each side) in ivory. Inside each of these, work a diamond, three squares wide on each side, using gold or orange. In between the large ivory diamonds, work large diamonds (five squares wide on each side) in gold or orange and, inside these, smaller diamonds in ivory. Continue the design to the edges of the space available. Fill the single-square spaces in the centre of each large diamond using assorted colours from the border.

9 Remove the tacking marking the edge of the square.

10 To make the cushion cover, start by cutting the silk fabric. If you are using a zip, cut two pieces measuring 50 x 27 cm (15⅝ x 10⅝ in.) and four pieces at 50 x 12 cm (15⅝ x 4¾ in.) If not, you will need one piece measuring 50 x 50 cm (15⅝ x 15⅝ in.) and four pieces measuring 50 x 12 cm (15⅝ x 4¾ in). All seam allowances are 2 cm (¾ in.). **Tip:** *Both silk and artificial silk fray easily, so now is a good time to secure the edges of all the pieces, most easily by using a zigzag stitch on your sewing machine.*

11 If you are using a zip, place the two larger pieces of silk fabric right sides together and stitch along one long edge for 5 cm (2 in.). Repeat from the other end of the edge. Tack in between the stitching. Press the seam open and centre the zip under the tacked part of the seam, with right side of the zip to wrong side of the seam. Pin and tack in place.

12 Fit the zipper foot to your sewing machine and stitch the zip in place, stitching down both sides and across the ends. Remove your tacking and check that the zip will open and close. You now have a 50 x 50 cm (15⅝ x 15⅝ in.) square of fabric, with a zip across the centre.

13 Both zipped and non-zipped covers are completed as follows. Remember to put the normal stitching foot back on your sewing machine. Press the embroidered fabric carefully and align it, along one edge, with one of the strips of silk/artificial silk material, right sides together, but with the back of the embroidered panel uppermost, so that you can see the edge of the embroidery. Stitch carefully along this exact edge. Join the two with a 2 cm (1 in.) seam allowance, taking care not to stitch into the seam allowance at each end. Repeat along all four sides of the embroidery, taking care not to catch adjoining strips in the stitching.

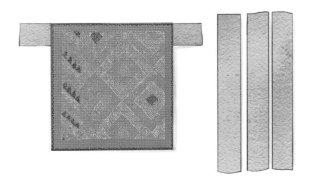

14 Now mitre the corners. Fold the embroidered square diagonally at one corner, wrong sides together, with the stitched edge strips hanging outside. Fold the top strip downwards, so that it forms a fold at right angles to the edge of the folded embroidery, and press lightly to make a crease. Unfold and stitch along the crease, taking care not to stitch beyond the hem of the embroidery. **Tip:** *This seam will be on the bias - take care not to stretch it as you stitch.* Trim the diagonal seam to 1 cm (⅜ in.) Repeat at all corners of the cover, and press the entire front.

15 Place each tassel on the right side of the cushion cover front, with 1 cm (⅜ in.) of the cord loop inside the seam allowance. Tack across the corner on the seam line.

16 Place the front and back of the cover right sides together. Fit the zipper foot on your sewing machine (allowing you to sew over the tassels). If you are using a zip closure on the cushion, open it a little way (so that you will be able to turn the cover right side out later), then stitch round all four sides. Turn the cover right side out, insert the cushion pad and close the zip.

17 If you are not using a zip, mark two points, 7 cm (2¾ in.) in from each corner, on one side. Stitch around all four sides, leaving the space between these two points unstitched. Turn the cover right side out, insert the cushion pad and, turning the loose seam allowances to the inside, **slip stitch** (see p.15) the cover closed.

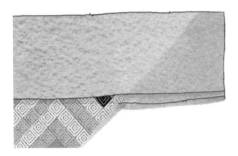

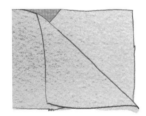

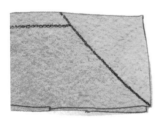

Now try...

Using the embroidered panel, or a smaller panel, for another project. It could feature as the front panel of a strong cotton tote bag, for example. If you use a fabric with a lower thread count, your design will be larger.

Charts for main motif (above) and border (below, optional)

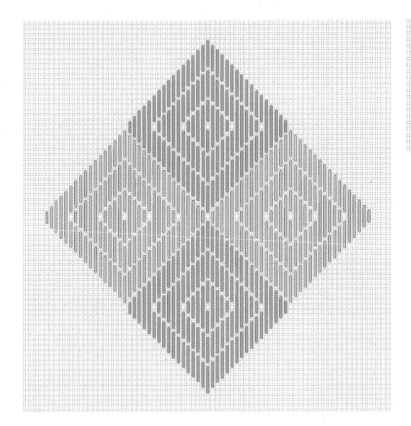

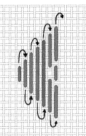

Stitch
direction

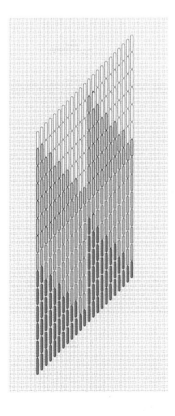

Stitch
direction

FREESTYLE

In 'freestyle' embroidery (the term embraces all non-counted handwork techniques), stitches may be worked freely or follow a design that has been printed, transferred or traced onto the background fabric; areas can be left unworked or the surface completely covered with embroidery. Almost any design can be interpreted in stitch, from naturalistic scenes to highly decorative patterning and, because no counting of threads is required, the fabrics available to the embroider include many different kinds of woven, and even non-woven, fabrics. A vast number of stitches can be employed and colour blending used to create realistic three-dimensional effects. Threads can also be laid onto the fabric surface and secured in place with a second thread (couching), a method commonly used in goldwork (see p.88).

Chinese robe (detail), late 18th century
Satin-weave silk embroidered with silk, length: 143.5 cm (56½ in.)
V&A: T.12–1950

EMBROIDERY

CREWELWORK

A form of surface embroidery at least 1,000 years old, crewelwork takes its name from the yarn used – a fine, 2-ply wool called crewel. Traditionally, the colourful, exuberant designs were worked on a closely woven linen or cotton background using a needle with a long, narrow eye. A wide range of stitches is used to outline and fill in the motifs, following patterns transferred on to the fabric, and to create beautiful shaded and textured effects. This style of rich, elaborate embroidery is often referred to as Jacobean crewelwork, though this is a misnomer, as the technique did not enjoy special popularity during the reign of James I of England (1603-25; James VI of Scotland from 1567).

Natural motifs
In the late seventeenth and early eighteenth centuries, crewelwork was fashionable for large domestic furnishings such as bed hangings and curtains. Designs originating in this period were heavily influenced by Indian chintzes, characterized by bright and exotic patterns of highly stylized flora and fauna. The 'Tree of Life' was a dominant motif and was readily taken up by English embroiderers, who enhanced the central tree's graceful twisting branches with all manner of fanciful leaves, flowers and fruits. Whimsical insects, birds and animals were also common additions to the imaginative cornucopia of stitched motifs. Today, contemporary designs interpreted in cotton, silk or wool threads are often used to make home and fashion accessories.

Curtain, 1660-1700
Linen and cotton twill embroidered
with crewel wool, 124.5 x 190.5 cm
(49 x 75 in.)
V&A: T.29-1932

Workbag, 1701–2

The construction of this large, linen-and-cotton workbag is simple: a single piece of fabric has been folded in half and the sides overstitched together, with a drawstring added as a closure. The chain-stitch crewelwork decoration and choice of colours, however – as is typical of eighteenth-century workbags of this kind – evince a high level of skill and reflect contemporary fashions in needlework. The twisting foliage that appears on both the front and back of the bag, and the ornate birds, were popular decorative devices in the period. The proud maker has initialled the bag: 'ER'.

Linen and cotton embroidered with crewel wool,
61 x 45 cm (24 x 17¾ in.)
V&A: T.166–1984

RASPBERRY PHONE POUCH

This little case – the perfect size for your smart phone, though it would also work as a make-up pouch or stationery case – is inspired by the Elizabethan workbag shown on pp.74–75. A simplified section of the 'Tree of Life' design worked on that bag – a popular motif in the period – has been used here, and offers an accessible introduction to the crewelwork tradition.

You will need

Yellow light- to medium-weight linen, 30 x 30 cm (12 x 12 in.)

Plain calico (unbleached cotton cloth), 15 x 30 cm (6 x 12 in.)

Cotton fabric of your choice (for bag lining and flap), 30 x 30 cm (12 x 12 in.)

Crewel wool, Appleton: one skein 222 (pale red); one skein 224 (mid red); one skein 226 (deep red); one skein 582 (brown); one skein 473 (yellow); one skein 407 (sea green); one skein 252 (pale green); one skein 254 (mid green); one skein 256 (deep green)

General sewing thread

Crewel/embroidery needle, size 7

Erasable marker

18 cm (7 in.) embroidery hoop

Embroidery, or other sharp, fine-pointed scissors

Pins

Optional

Sewing machine

Two press studs (snaps), 6 mm (¼ in.)

Project by Sarah Homfray

How to make

1 Cut the linen fabric into two pieces, each 15 x 30 cm (6 x 12 in.). Trace the design template (p.81) onto one of your pieces of linen fabric as per the instructions on p.13, and set the other piece aside.

2 Place your piece of calico on a flat surface and the marked linen directly over the top, face up. Place the two over the inner ring of your embroidery hoop and push the outer hoop down over the top, to secure the layers of fabric as tightly as possible. You will work the embroidery through both layers simultaneously.

3 Use the stitch plan (right) and the photograph (p.77) to help you work colours and stitches throughout. First, outline the berry segments, starting with the bottom segment, in two rows of **split stitch** (see p.14), the first in pale red and the second in mid red. Fill the remaining space with French knots in deep red.

4 Next work the brown vein down the large berry bud (B) in **stem stitch** (see p.14) and the outline in the same using deep red. Work a second row inside this in the mid red and a final row in pale red.

5 Work the small berry bud (E) in the same way as for B.

6 Next, work the upper leaf (A) in rows of **chain stitch** (see p.15), starting from the outside in the yellow. Work through the colours inside each previous row: pale green, mid green, deep green and sea green. Fill in any space left with the sea green, leaving space for the stem. Work the vein in chain stitch in brown.

7 Work the large curved leaf (C) in the same way as the upper leaf in rows of chain stitch, shading from sea green on the left-hand side through to the pale green. Use yellow and pale green for the right-hand side.

Stitch diagram

Key
1 Split stitch
2 Chain stitch
3 Stem stitch
4 French knot
5 Satin stitch

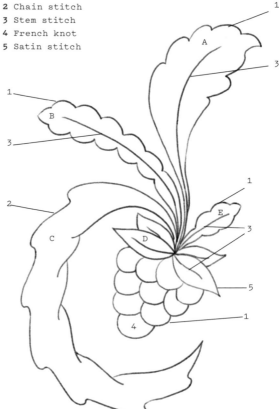

8 To finish, work the stem of the berry leaves (D) in stem stitch in yellow. Using mid green, work a second row around the yellow vein on the lower two leaves only. Work around the leaves themselves in **satin stitch** (see p.15) using the sea green. Start with the back two leaves, then work the front two.

9 Remove your finished embroidery from the frame and trim to 12 x 19 cm (4¾ x 7½ in.), centring your design. **Note:** *The finished case is 10 x 17 cm (4 x 6¾ in.). This includes a 1 cm (⅜ in.) seam allowance all the way around.*

Start by stitching the pink berry, and then move on to the leaves.

10 Place the embroidered linen piece and the second piece of linen fabric together, right sides facing, and pin. Trim the second piece to match the embroidered piece. Hand or machine stitch three sides as shown below with a 1 cm (⅜ in.) seam allowance, leaving the top open. Clip the corners of the fabric and turn out, so that you have a 'bag', and press.

11 Make another bag out of your chosen lining fabric. Cut a piece of fabric 23 x 19 cm (9 x 7½ in.). Fold the fabric in half and stitch two sides as shown below. The lining should be 6 mm (¼ in.) smaller all the way around so that it fits inside the bag, so adjust your seam allowance accordingly. Clip off the corners, but leave the lining inside out. Make a small tab in the same way with your remaining lining fabric. Turn right side out.

12 Turn over the top edge of the embroidered pouch bag twice, pin and press into place. Repeat for the lining.

13 Place the lining inside the pouch and position the raw end of the tab between the seams of the two bags. Pin everything in place and sew around the top of the pouch, catching in the tab, either overcasting by hand or topstitching by machine. Add press studs for a fastening if you wish.

Add press studs to your pouch and tab if you require a more secure closure.

Design template

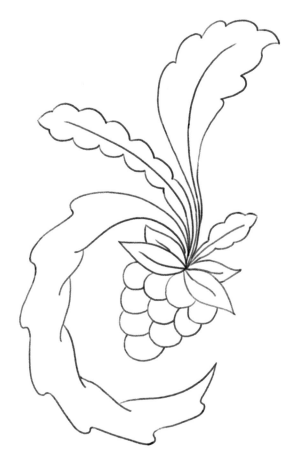

Template shown at 100%

Now try...

Altering the dimensions of the made-up bag
to make larger bags and modifying the design,
for example with a zip or larger flap. You can
also modify the design itself by using a different
palette of colours.

CHINESE SILK

Embroidery (*xiu*) has been known in China for thousands of years, and most traditional work is made in silk. A wide range of time-honoured designs — figurative motifs, such as flowers, birds and animals, and geometric or abstract patterns — are known. A variety of stitches are used, but long-and-short, satin and padded stitches are common. Untwisted (flat) silk threads give a rich sheen and, when combined with padded stitching, create wonderful three-dimensional effects. Twisted threads are stronger and give bolder lines, but still have a delightful lustre.

Styles of embroidery

There are four distinct regional styles of Chinese embroidery. *Shu xiu* comes from the southwest province of Sichuan, and the motifs used are mostly from the natural world. From the eastern coastal province of Jiangsu, the colours of *Su xiu* are more naturalistic. Associated with Hunan province in south-central China, *Xiang xiu* is notable for emulating other Chinese art forms — mostly paintings, but also engravings and calligraphy. *Yue xiu*, from Guangdong, China's southernmost coastal province, combines elements of the other styles. Stylistically, it is characterized by the use of strong colours, with no attempt to produce an illusion of depth; mythical creatures such as dragons and phoenixes are common motifs.

Panel (detail), 18th century
Satin-weave silk embroidered with silk and gold threads, 83.8 x 50.8 cm (33 x 20 in.)
V&A: T.171-1948

Jacket, 1915

The motifs in the project overleaf were inspired by the polychrome silk embroidery on this child's jacket, made in Jinan, China. Satin-weave silk has been embellished with satin stitch and overlaid floats, and with seed stitch, stem stitch and gold couching, to form a design showing figures surrounded by flowers. Made domestically, as part of a complete ensemble (including shoes), the jacket was a gift to a young mother – it is a custom in China to present a child with red and green clothes bearing auspicious motifs – but was considered too precious ever to be worn.

Satin-weave silk with embroidery, 44.5 x 67 cm
(17½ x 26⅜ in.; across shoulders)
V&A: FE.12–1986

FLORAL DENIM EMBROIDERY

These floral motifs can be stitched onto any fabric surface as an embellishment; worked on denim, they can be used to customize jeans, a jacket (as here), or any garment you choose! Experiment with design placement to make your own, unique composition. Inspired by traditional floral motifs from Chinese silk embroidery, the motifs are worked in just three stitches: padded satin stitch, French knots and stem stitch. We've recommended using stranded cotton (floss) rather than silk, for durability and easy care. You can use the thread colours specified here or choose your own.

You will need

Denim garment (our jacket is a UK size 10/ US size 6)
DMC stranded cotton (floss): one skein 704 (lime green); one skein 601 (bright pink); one skein 700 (dark green); one skein 597 (light blue); one skein 321 (red); one skein 'blanc' (white)
Embroidery needle, size 9
Tracing paper
Pen or pencil
Dressmaker's carbon paper
Ballpoint pen
Pale watercolour pencil or quilter's pencil/washable marker
Embroidery, or other sharp, fine-pointed scissors

Project by Rachel Doyle

How to make

Position the motifs as on the template or try different placements to fit the area you are stitching.

1 Trace the design templates (opposite) onto tracing paper (see p.13) in your chosen arrangement. If you are working on a garment, check that the design will fit in the area chosen.

2 Once you are happy with the placement, cut a piece of dressmaker's carbon paper to the same approximate size as your design area and sandwich it between your tracing and the denim fabric. Working on a flat surface, trace over your design using a ballpoint pen to transfer it to the denim. Go over the design lines with a pale water-colour pencil if they are not clear enough.

3 Work the **padded satin stitch** (see p.15) areas first (see stitch diagram, opposite). Choose your first thread colour and cut off a short length, no more than 30 cm (12 in.). Separate two strands of the cotton, thread them into your embroidery needle and knot the end. Start each thread with a knot on top of the work and two small securing stitches within the design area. Once you start the decorative stitching, you can cut the knot away.

4 Each padded satin stitch area is worked with long stitches running across the entire shape. Keep the stitches close together and parallel. Then work a second set of stitches in the same way over the top, at ninety degrees to the first. End all threads by weaving in on the back of the embroidery.

5 Next work the **stem stitch** (see p.14, for the stems and leaf veins), using two strands of thread. The stitch can be worked as one, two or three rows, depending on the thickness of the line you would like to achieve. It is worked on top of the satin stitch of the leaves.

6 Finally, **French knots** (see p.16) are packed closely together to fill the remaining areas. Work these stitches using three strands of thread.

Now try...

Enlarging or reducing the motifs provided here to create your own unique interpretation. The colours and stitch placements could be changed or rearranged and the motifs worked in just one or two colours.

Design template and stitch diagram

Key
1 Padded satin stitch
2 Stem stitch
3 French knots

Template shown at 100%

GOLDWORK

Embroidery has been worked in precious threads for at least 2,000 years. Originally executed in pure gold and silver, such work has always been associated with wealth and status. For maximum effect with minimum waste, couching (see p.16) is the principal method used – it is the primary technique in the lavish Dior evening dress shown opposite. Incorporated alongside other embroidery techniques, and embellished with gems, sequins and beads, wonderfully extravagant effects can be produced. Traditional goldwork remains an important element of religious, military and ceremonial regalia. Modern domestic embroiderers, meanwhile, have access to affordable synthetic threads in a wide range of metallic colours. By combining these with other contemporary materials and non-traditional methods, exciting new designs can be created.

Medieval brilliance

Between 1250 and 1350, goldwork in England reached remarkable heights of artistry and technical accomplishment in the form of embroidery known as *opus anglicanum* (Latin for 'English work'). Produced mostly by professional embroiderers in London workshops – medieval England's creative hub – these gloriously opulent embroideries were highly prized and sought after all across Europe. Elaborate imagery was contained within a narrative framework – often, in an ecclesiastical context, depicting scenes from the Bible. After England's Reformation in the sixteenth century, many medieval embroideries were either taken apart to recover the precious materials or exported to Catholic countries. A growth of interest in medieval art in the nineteenth century led to the rediscovery of *opus anglicanum*.

Christian Dior (with embroidery by Bodin Brossin), 'H-line' dress, 1954-55
Satin embroidered with silver and gold threads, waist: 59 cm (23¼ in.)
V&A: T.12&A-1977

Burse, 1320-30
Linen embroidered with silver-gilt and silk threads, 26 x 54 cm (10¼ x 21¼ in.)
V&A: T.62-1936

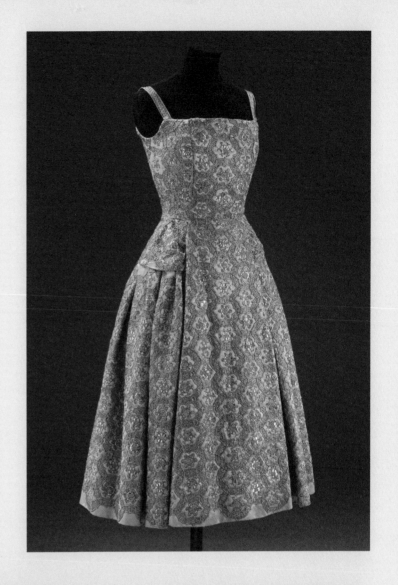

The Steeple Aston Cope, 1330–40

This magnificent example of *opus anglicanum* survives in the form of altar furnishings, having at some point (probably at the time of the Reformation) been cut up and rearranged. Originally part of a cope – a large, semicircular cape-like ecclesiastical vestment worn by higher-ranking clergy – the embroidered pieces here have been worked on a woven silk twill in the characteristic stitches of *opus anglicanum*: underside couching (using gilded silver thread) and split stitch (using silk). Oak and ivy branches structure the design, which features scenes from the lives of the saints, and of Christ and the Virgin. Note the striped stockings of the saints' torturers (opposite) – a symbol of pride.

Woven silk embroidered with silver-gilt and silver thread and coloured silks, 89 x 285 cm (35 x 112¼ in; frontal); 141 x 160 cm (55½ x 63 in.; dossal)
The Rector and Churchwardens of St Peter and St Paul, Steeple Aston (Oxfordshire), on loan to the Victoria and Albert Museum, London, since 1905

GREEN MAN SEW-ON PATCH

The defining techniques of *opus anglicanum* (see p.88) were split-stitch shading and underside couching. Both are used to create this sew-on 'Green Man' patch, the motif for which was inspired by the leaf-masks embroidered on the Steeple Aston Cope, shown on pp.90–91. A symbol of growth and rebirth, the 'Green Man' has been found all over the world, in architecture and literature as well as textiles.

You will need

Green light- to medium-weight cotton or linen fabric, 20 x 20 cm (8 x 8 in.)
Plain calico (unbleached cotton cloth) or other cotton backing fabric, 20 x 20 cm (8 x 8 in.)
Heavy interfacing (such as Pelmet Vilene or Pellon 50 Heavyweight Stabilizer), 10 x 10 cm (4 x 4 in.)
DMC stranded cotton (floss): 3774 (neutral), 809 (blue), 'blanc' (white), 3371 (brown), 3345 (green)
DMC Metallic Pearl thread, brilliant gold (5282)
DMC Diamant couching thread, gold
100% linen thread, Gutermann 4013, for underside couching and gathering patch
General sewing thread, to match green fabric
Embroidery needle, size 10
Crewel/embroidery needle, size 5
Erasable marker
13 cm (5 in.) embroidery hoop
Embroidery, or other sharp, fine-pointed scissors

Project by Sarah Homfray

How to make

1 Trace the design template opposite and transfer to your green embroidery fabric (see p.13), centring the design.

2 Lay your embroidery fabric over the backing fabric and secure both in your embroidery hoop.

3 Using the stitch direction guide opposite for the whole of the face, stitch the eyes first. Work **satin stitch** (see p.15) in the pupil, using one strand of the brown thread and the size 10 embroidery needle. The thread consists of six strands; cut a forearm-length piece of thread, separate the ends and pull one strand out straight upwards.

4 Work one row of **split stitch** (see p.14) around the pupils, using one strand of the blue cotton. Work the rest of the eyes in rows of split stitch, using one strand of the white stranded cotton.

5 Work the face around the eyes in split stitch, using two strands of the neutral stranded cotton.

6 Work the background around the mouth details in two strands of the neutral colour. Work the mouth details in the brown cotton, using small **fly stitches** (see p.16) to create the shapes. Work the nose last, in two strands of the neutral colour.

7 Work the outline of the gold leaves in **couching** (see p.16), using the Metallic Pearl thread and couching it down with one strand of the green stranded thread. Start at one of the leaf tips, near the base. If you need to stop and start a thread, do so on one of the leaf points: thread the Metallic Pearl into your crewel needle and take it through to the back of the fabric to finish, then work a few stitches over it with the Diamant thread to hold it in place. Work couching around the face outline in the gold Metallic Pearl, couching down with the gold Diamant thread.

Work the face first, following the stitch direction guide.

8 Work the leaf veins in **underside couching** (see p.16) using six strands of the green stranded thread, couched down using linen thread in the size 5 crewel needle. Start at the face, working outwards; work all of the couching and then take the ends through to the back, fastening as before.

9 Work a row of underside couching around the edge of the whole design, again using six strands of the green stranded cotton.

10 To make the patch base, cut a circle 8 cm (3⅛ in.) in diameter out of the heavy interfacing.

11 Turn your embroidery over and cut away the backing fabric to within 6 mm (¼ in.) of the edge of the embroidery. Cut the embroidery fabric to within 3 cm (1⅛ in.) of the edge of the cut backing. (Place the interfacing circle in the centre and check that there is plenty of fabric to fold over the edge of the interfacing before you cut!)

12 Work **running stitch** (see p.14) 1 cm (⅜ in.) in from the edge of the fabric with the linen thread, leaving both ends loose. Place the interfacing circle on the back of the stitching and pull the linen thread around the interfacing to pull the fabric into a circle. Tie the two linen threads together tightly. Press the edges of your circle flat.

Now try...

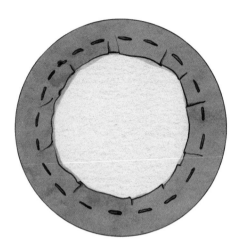

Playing around with the fabric and thread colours to change the appearance of your Green Man; try a palette of rich russet reds for an autumnal effect!

13 Sew into place on your chosen item using a **slip stitch** (see p.15) and sewing thread to match your green fabric.

Design template

Template shown at 100%

Stitch direction guide

ART NEEDLEWORK

'Art needlework' is the name given to a style of
embroidery that became popular in Europe and North
America in the later nineteenth century. Good design
was combined with skill and invention in stitch;
originality in the selection and arrangement of colours;
and the use of suitable, carefully chosen materials.
Art needleworkers used a small number of traditional
embroidery stitches: primarily long-and-short, satin,
stem, split, French knots, darning and couching, worked
in naturally dyed wools and silks, and metal threads, on
a variety of backgrounds, including linen, cotton, silk
and wool.

Arts and Crafts
The English designer William Morris (1834-96) championed
art needlework through his firm Morris & Co. He was a
key figure in the Arts and Crafts movement, which began
in Britain around 1880 and quickly spread to North
America, continental Europe and Japan. The movement
advocated the revival of traditional handicrafts, of
which art needlework is just one example. The Victorian
obsession with Berlin woolwork (see p.30) had eclipsed
most other forms of embroidery, but Morris thought this
type of canvas shading, worked in cross or tent stitch
from mass-produced patterns in bright synthetic colours,
was responsible for the decline in needle skills. In
reaction to this, he promoted traditional techniques in
his embroidery designs, which were usually inspired by
nature and often influenced by historic textiles from
Italy, Iran (then Persia) and Turkey. The piece shown
opposite is the work of Morris's daughter, May, a skilled
embroiderer and designer in her own right, who began
running the embroidery section of Morris & Co. in 1885.

'Orange Tree', designed and
embroidered by May Morris,
possibly late 1890s
Silks on linen, 41.8 x 43.5 cm
(16½ x 17⅛ in.)
William Morris Society: T33.
Bequeathed by Helena
Stephenson, 1970.

Wall hanging, made 1877–1900 (designed 1877)

This embroidered panel – showing a repeated, stylized design of blue-and-brown artichoke heads and leaves – has been worked in crewel wools on linen, using long-and-short, stem and satin stitch, and French knots. It belongs to a set designed and worked to hang at Smeaton Manor, in Northallerton, North Yorkshire. The embroiderer, Mrs Ada Phoebe Godman, lived at Smeaton and commissioned designer William Morris to produce the templates for her to work – the finished hangings took more than 20 years to complete. The design has a traditional structure and evidences Morris's preoccupation in the 1870s and 1880s with Middle-Eastern and early Italian silks and velvets.

Linen embroidered with crewel wools, 207.5 x 153 cm (81¾ x 60¼ in.)
V&A: T.166–1978

ARTICHOKE CUSHION

Taking an artichoke head motif from William Morris's design for the wall hangings at Smeaton Manor, Northallerton (see p.98), this project will teach you how to create an elegant embroidery in Morris's original colour palette of rich blues, greens and browns. This timeless design is made up into a square cushion here, but could equally be framed as a work of art in its own right.

You will need

Two pieces of plain-weave, natural-coloured linen, each 34 x 34 cm (13½ x 13½ in.)

Navy plaited braid for trim, 140 cm (55 in.)

Cushion pad (pillow form), 30 x 30 cm (12 x 12 in.)

Soie d'Alger thread, Au Ver à Soie: one skein 4541 (beige); one skein 4543 (cinnamon); one skein 4545 (brown); one skein 3723 (light green), one skein 3724 (mid green); one skein 3725 (dark green); one skein 4140 (pale blue); one skein 1713 (mid blue); one skein 1436 (navy); two skeins 1434 (dark blue)

Tacking (basting) thread

General sewing thread, to match linen ground

Crewel needle, size 7

Hand-sewing needle

Embroidery, or other sharp, fine-pointed scissors

20 cm (8 in.) embroidery hoop, or 45 cm (18 in.) rectangular frame

Pencil

Fabric scissors

Tape measure

Pins

Optional

Sewing machine

Zipper foot

Project by Dr Lynn Hulse

How to make

1 Trace the template on p.107 and transfer the design, positioning the motif in the centre of one of the pieces of linen fabric (see p.13). Secure your fabric in an embroidery hoop or rectangular frame.

2 Stitch the central artichoke bud. The six leaves are worked in long-and-short stitch (see right) using two strands of pale blue, then two strands of mid blue. The leaves are worked in the order indicated in the diagram below.

Tip: *When working long-and-short stitch, don't make the stitches too small. Remember, up to half of each stitch will be hidden on working the next row (see right). Forming the stitches over a laying tool - a blunt, needle-like tool (you could use a large sewing needle intended for woollens) - can help to prevent the threads twisting and to keep the strands perfectly tensioned and lying parallel on the fabric.*

3 Start with leaf 1. The first row is worked in pale blue. Starting at the centre, bring the needle up inside the leaf shape and down over the design outline to make a long stitch (A-B, below). The stitches in this first row vary in length, alternating between long and short, until the end of the line is reached and one half of the row is complete with none of the fabric showing through the stitching (A-B, C-D, E-F, and so on). This is long-and-short stitch. Work in exactly the same way in the opposite direction.

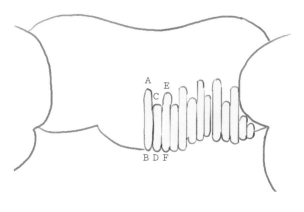

4 The second row is worked using mid blue. Bring the needle up **through** the stitches in the first row and down into the fabric (a-b, c-d, e-f, and so on). Again, start at the centre of the row and work in one direction to the end of the line; return to the centre and continue in the opposite direction. **Note:** *The stitches in this second row are even in length but the 'tops' and 'bottoms' are staggered to create a soft blended effect.*

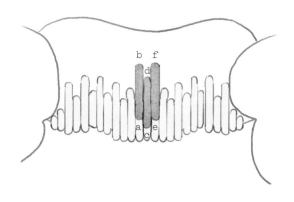

5 Work the third row in mid blue. Make sure the 'bottoms' of the stitches in this row finish on and cover the design outline.

6 Work the rest of the bud in the same manner, always starting with the lightest colour and adjusting the number of rows stitched in each colour to fit the size of the leaf shape. In order to create some contrast in the shading at the base of the bud, the final row in leaf 4 is worked using one strand each of mid blue and dark blue. **Tip:** *As the leaf shape reduces in size, the number of stitches in each row will decrease also. It is better to fan out the stitches at the top of these shorter rows and bring the bottoms closer together towards the base of the leaf.*

7 The centre of the bud is filled with **French knots** (see p.15) using three strands of brown. Wrap the thread only once around the needle.

8 The lower four leaves are worked in long-and-short stitch using dark green, mid green, light green, beige, cinnamon and brown. The leaves are stitched in the order indicated in the diagram below. **Tip:** *To ensure that the stitches lie at an angle of approximately 45° to the centre vein, mark guidelines in pencil on each leaf before commencing work, as shown below.*

9 Start with leaf 1. The first row is worked in one strand each of dark green and mid green. The stitches forming the spiky tip are created by bringing the needle up inside the shape and back down over the design outline. Working from the centre outwards, place stitches to either side to fill the tip.

10 Continue working up the left-hand side of the leaf, making sure that the stitches cover the design outline and angle towards the centre vein. As before, the stitches in this first row vary in length, alternating between long and short, until the end of the line is reached and one half of the leaf is complete.

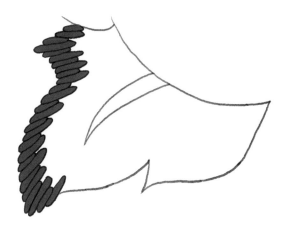

11 The second row is stitched using two strands of mid green. Continuing to work up the left-hand side of the leaf, bring the needle up through the stitches in the first row and back down into the shape, as before. As with the artichoke bud, the stitches in this and all subsequent rows are even in length but the 'tops' and 'bottoms' are staggered.

Wrapping the hoop with fabric will protect your linen from marking.

12 Work the third row in two strands of light green; the fourth row in one strand each of beige and cinnamon; and the fifth row in two strands of cinnamon, making sure this time that the 'bottoms' of the stitches in this final row terminate on the outline of the centre vein.

13 Repeat steps 10-12 up the right-hand side to fill the whole leaf shape.

14 The centre vein is outlined in **split stitch** (see p.14) using two strands of brown. Ensure that the tip has a sharp point before returning down the other side of the vein. The centre is left unfilled to expose the fabric.

15 The upper four leaves are worked in long-and-short stitch in mid blue, dark blue, navy, beige, cinnamon and brown. The upper leaves are stitched in exactly the same way as the lower. The first row is worked in one strand each of dark blue and navy; the second row in two strands of dark blue; the third row in two strands of mid blue; the fourth row in one strand each of beige and cinnamon; and the fifth and final row in two strands of cinnamon. The centre vein is outlined in split stitch using two strands of brown.

16 The undersides of the upper leaves are worked in long-and-short stitch using one strand each of beige and cinnamon.

17 The calyx (at the bottom) is worked in long-and-short stitch, starting at the top, using two strands each of mid green and light green. The first and second rows are worked in mid green and the third and final row in light green.

18 When the stitching in each area is complete, the outlines are worked in split stitch as follows: the leaves of the artichoke bud in two strands of dark blue; the upper outer leaves in two strands of navy; the lower outer leaves and the calyx in two strands of dark green.

19 Pin the plaited braid around the edge of the right side of the back cushion cover in line with the 2 cm (¾ in.) seam allowance. Allow an extra few centimetres of cord for the overlap, which should lie at the mid point on the lower edge of the cover. Cut slits into the seam allowance of the braid at the corners so that it sits flat and smooth. Tack (baste) in place with a contrasting coloured thread. It is impossible to achieve a 90-degree corner with braid so the finished cushion cover will have slightly rounded corners.

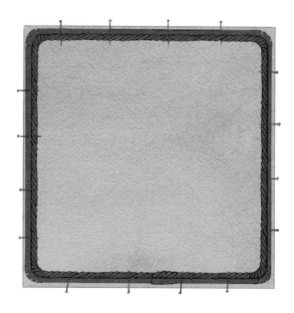

20 If you are using a sewing machine to stitch the cover, use a zipper foot to sew on the plaited braid, stitching up close to the braid and taking extra care on the corners. Alternatively, sew by hand using **backstitch** (see p.14). At the point where the braid overlaps, sew straight across. Trim the excess braid so that the edges are in line with the edge of the fabric. Remove the tacking thread.

The outlines are worked in split stitch to finish off the design.

21 Pin the front and back pieces right sides together and tack in place. Stitch together on the 2 cm (¾ in.) seam allowance close to the piping, sewing over the overlap in the cord. Leave a 20 cm (8 in.) gap down one side of the cover through which to insert the cushion pad. Trim the corners to remove any excess fabric and remove the tacking thread.

22 Turn the cover right side out and gently poke out the corners. Insert cushion pad and **slip stitch** (see p.15) the opening.

Now try...

Adapting this design for other needlework techniques, exchanging materials and a few key stitches. The easiest version might be canvas work; use Soie d'Alger silks or Fine D'Aubusson wools on a 22- or 25-count canvas. The entire design can be worked in tent stitch, as well as the background.

Design template

Template shown at 100%

WHITE WORK

A tradition in many countries, whitework is the name given specifically to white embroidery on white fabric (it comprises freestyle, counted-thread and canvas-work embroidery techniques). The stitching must be smooth and even, which requires fine needle skills, and therefore, historically, much whitework was produced professionally. As with other forms of embroidery, however, in the mid- to late nineteenth century it became a fashionable pastime for middle-class European and American ladies. Many forms – such as Hardanger, beautiful counted-thread work from Norway – include open spaces that have been cut out or created by drawing threads out of the fabric. As a result, whitework is often associated with lacy patterns. Whitework is commonly used for ecclesiastical linens and garments, as well as christening wear and trimmings.

Cap, 18th century
Linen with drawn-thread work and quilting, circumference: 57.5 cm (22⅝ in.)
V&A: CIRC.966–1923

BRODERIE ANGLAISE

Broderie anglaise is a simple type of cutwork.
Also known as eyelet embroidery, the work consists
of holes with overcast edges – often circular
or oval, and of varying sizes – which create
a lace-like effect. The background fabric needs
to be closely woven, so fabrics such as cotton
cambric, cotton lawn and fine linen are often
used, along with matching thread for the embroidery.
Designs frequently comprise floral motifs, whose
formations lend themselves to the circular and
oval perforations. In earlier pieces, no surface
embroidery was used, with stalks and leaves
created from eyelets of diminishing sizes.
By the mid-nineteenth century, however, simple
embroidery stitches were used to add further
definition to the patterns, in areas such as
stems and vines. Scalloped edges, finished with
buttonhole stitch, are a typical feature.

A decorative flourish

Believed to have originated in eastern Europe
in the sixteenth century, this technique remains
most closely associated with England – broderie
anglaise is French for 'English embroidery'.
A delightful decoration, it was commonly used
to trim baby clothes, dresses, nightclothes and
underclothes, and household linens. It was also
used to make caps and bonnets. Traditional
motifs adapt beautifully to modern clothing
and accessories; once produced entirely by
hand, these are now usually machine-made.

Child's coat, 1879
Cotton with embroidery and
quilting, length: 71 cm (28 in.)
V&A: T.162-1962

Child's pinafore, c.1918

This simple cotton garment features a repeating floral pattern in broderie anglaise. Although the pattern itself is simple, it has been artfully applied on various areas of the garment, and with variations in orientation and complexity, so that the final garment, though made of white cotton, looks relatively lavish.

Cotton with machine-made embroidery
V&A: MISC.211–1979

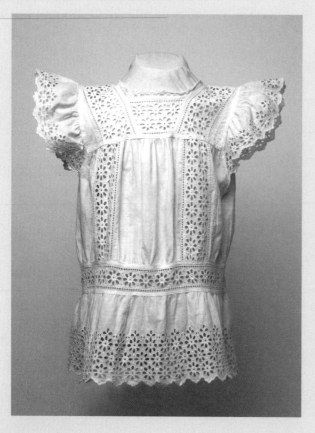 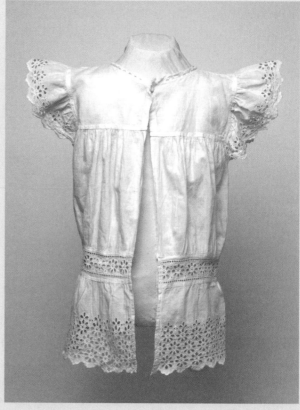

FLORAL BUNTING

These broderie anglaise flags can be used to decorate a room, window or door – perhaps to celebrate a special event. Round and oval eyelets create delicate, white-cotton floral details on white linen, edged with buttonhole stitch. Simply stitch additional flags to make this five-flag bunting longer.

You will need

Fine white linen (45 thread count or higher) or cotton fabric, 55 x 30 cm (20 x 12 in.)

White ribbon (1 cm/⅜ in. wide), 114 cm (45 in.)

One skein stranded cotton (floss), white

Embroidery needle, size 9

Blue quilting pencil

Embroidery, or other sharp, fine-pointed scissors

Pins

15 cm (6 in.) embroidery hoop

Stiletto or knitting needle, 5 mm (US size 8)

Baby wipes

Project by Lucy Barter

How to make

1 Trace the design template (see p.119) and transfer the design to your fabric (see p.13). Position the first of the five flags in the centre of your fabric and trace using a blue quilter's pencil. Trace each of the flags in turn, allowing a 2 cm (1 in.) gap between each flag.

2 Position the fabric in an embroidery hoop, centring the first flag within the hoop area.

3 Cut a forearm's length of stranded cotton (floss). Separate two strands from the rest and thread into the needle. Tie a small knot at the end of the thread.

4 Work each flag in the following sequence: leaves, stem, eyelets, edging. Starting on one leaf, go down through the fabric, a short distance away from the design outline, leaving your knot on top (this will be cut off later). Work small **running stitches** (see p.14) along the outline of the shape, then go around the shape a second time, filling the gaps of the previous running stitches, to make a continuous line.

Stitch diagram

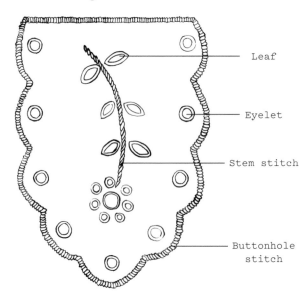

Leaf

Eyelet

Stem stitch

Buttonhole stitch

5 Once you have stitched around twice, bring the needle and thread up as close as possible to the outside edge of the running stitch, ready to overcast the leaf.

6 Before starting the overcasting, make a small hole in the centre of the leaf shape with the stiletto or knitting needle. Then take your embroidery scissors and cut little slits from the centre to the left and then the right of the hole towards the tip of the leaf.

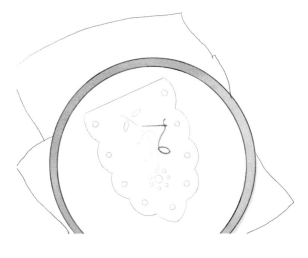

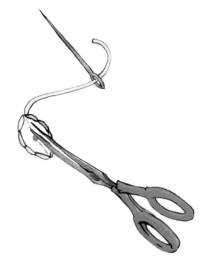

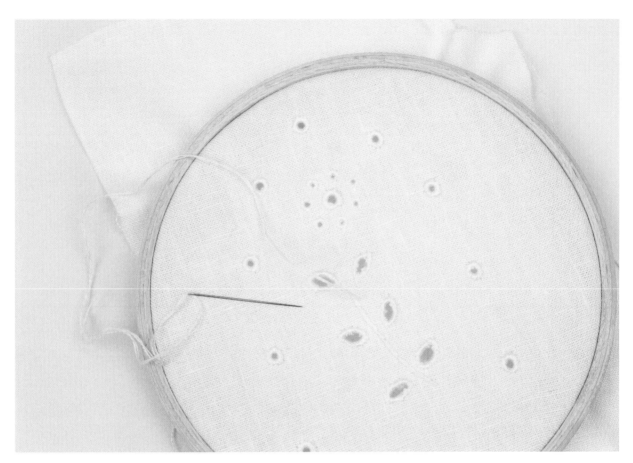

Work each of the leaves in turn, and then the eyelets, before working the central stem.

7 Start to overcast the running stitch by taking the needle down into the hole and back up on the outside of the running stitch, each time pulling tight to open up the hole. **Tip:** *It is a good idea to keep washing your hands when working with white thread on white fabric. It's good to have a packet of baby wipes on hand!*

8 Work around the whole shape, finishing on the reverse side of the work by slipping the needle under the stitches, directly beside where the needle went down. Cut off the remaining thread and the knot and tail of the starting thread. Repeat this process for each leaf.

9 The round eyelets are worked in the same manner as the leaves; the smaller eyelets only need to have a hole punched at the centre, while the larger ones will need a few slits cut in an X shape so that the hole can be opened wider. The small eyelets are close together and can be stitched with the same thread, just carry it across on the back of the work.

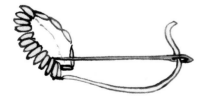

Sew flags onto the ribbon at regular intervals.

10 Work **stem stitch** (see p.14) from the flower head to the end of the stem, using two strands of thread. Start the thread with a knot on top, work two small holding stitches on the outline to fasten the thread and then stitch the stem over the top of these. Weave the tail through the stitches on the back of the work to fasten off.

11 Using two strands of thread, work **blanket/buttonhole stitch** (see p.15) round the edge of the flag. Again, start with a knot on the front of the work and two small holding stitches at the edge of the buttonhole area, which will be covered by your stitches. Work even-length stitches around the entire flag. To end one thread before starting another, weave the end though the back of the buttonhole stitches and cut the tail away. Start again, on the edge, with two holding stitches, and bring the needle up in the last loop of the previous stitch.

12 Once all the flags have been edged with buttonhole stitch, cut each one from the fabric, leaving a small allowance around the edge. On each flag, trim this allowance back to the very edge of the buttonhole stitch, using embroidery scissors and being careful not to cut into the stitches. Use your fingernail to dislodge any loose fibres and trim them away.

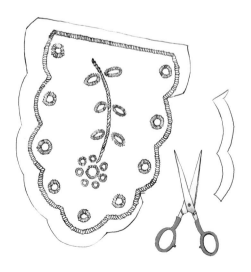

13 The flags are now ready to attach to your ribbon. Pin the flags in position evenly, lining up the top of each flag with the top edge of the ribbon. Using a single strand of the cotton thread, stitch each flag in place with running stitch, securing each end with a couple of overcasting stitches.

14 You can press the bunting with a warm iron from the back, using a towel underneath so as not to flatten your embroidery. Now it's ready to hang!

Now try...

Making longer bunting, adding flags made out of vintage printed or embroidered handkerchiefs alongside your own, handmade flags. Stitch a buttonhole edge around one corner of the handkerchief, cut out and stitch to the ribbon in the same way. You can also experiment with sewing the eyelets and buttonhole stitch in coloured threads – white is traditional, but not obligatory!

Design template

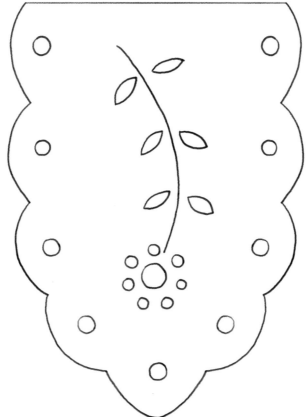

Template shown at 100%

MOUNTMELLICK

Unlike many other forms of whitework, Mountmellick does not include open spaces. It is, instead, a three-dimensional form of embroidery, with stitches planned so as to lie on the fabric's surface with as little thread as possible on the underside. Traditionally, large-scale, naturalistic designs were worked in knitting cotton of varying thicknesses on a heavy cotton ground. To balance the textured embroidery, the edges were generally finished with a heavy fringe; these sturdy fabrics and threads meant that the technique was employed to decorate household items such as bedspreads and tablecloths. Worked with finer materials, Mountmellick can be used to embellish special-occasion items such as wedding-ring pillows or christening robes.

The rise and fall of a craft

One of the few needlework techniques native to Ireland, Mountmellick is named after the town where it was said to have been introduced by a woman named Johanna Carter. She ran a small school teaching poor girls and women to sew as a means of supporting themselves. The materials used were manufactured locally, and designs were originally inspired by plants and flowers growing along the banks of the town's river. Mountmellick was taken up across Ireland, but by the mid-nineteenth century it had declined in popularity. In around 1880, a Mrs Millner started an Industrial Association at Mountmellick with the aim of developing it as a local industry. The London publisher Walter Weldon printed four volumes on the subject, and the technique had a revival as a hobby for middle-class ladies. The craft then almost died out again. In the 1970s, Sister Teresa Margaret McCarthy, a nun in Mountmellick's convent, revitalized the traditional skills.

Marèe Maher, tea cloth, 1989
Private collection

Marèe Maher, embroidery
sample, 2013
Private collection

Sachet, c.1880

Belonging to the second wave of Mountmellick's popularity, in the 1880s and 1890s, this handkerchief sachet features a delicate design of sprays of lilac and columbine. This main motif is worked in satin, stem and buttonhole stitching, while the scalloped borders also include French and bullion knots. The sachet is edged with cotton bobbin lace in a torchon pattern, which, although probably not made in Mountmellick, may well be contemporary with the sachet and added when it was made.

Cotton with whitework embroidery, 34.3 x 43.2 cm (13.5 x 17 in.)
V&A: T.100–1963

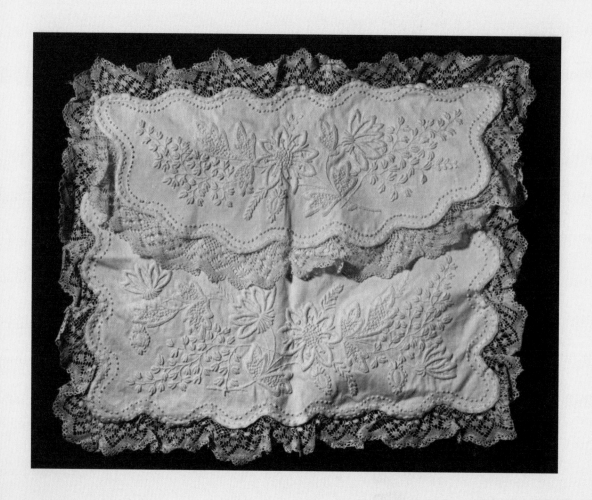

DECORATIVE COLLAR

This project is inspired by the 1880 handkerchief sachet on pp.122–23, with its lilac and columbine design, but updated to create a striking and contemporary accessory. Match the collar with white, or with bold colours to offset the delicate, white Mountmellick embroidery, worked in a variety of stitches on smooth, heavyweight cotton satin fabric.

You will need

White, smooth, heavyweight cotton, such as satin jean, twill or duck, 40 x 40 cm (16 x 16 in.)

Fabric for lining, 40 x 40 cm (16 x 16 in.) - ideally satin jean, but lighter fabrics, for example cotton lawn, could be used if interfaced

White satin ribbon (1 cm/⅜ in. wide), 60 cm (24 in.)

10 m (11 yd) white Mountmellick thread, size 3; or 1 skein white coton à broder, size 16

Chenille needle, size 18

Blue quilter's pencil

Embroidery, or other sharp, fine-pointed scissors

Baby wipes

25 cm (10 in.) embroidery hoop

Pins

Fabric stabilizer spray

Optional

Hand-sewing needle

General sewing thread, white

Iron-on interfacing

Project by Lucy Barter

How to make

Stitch diagram

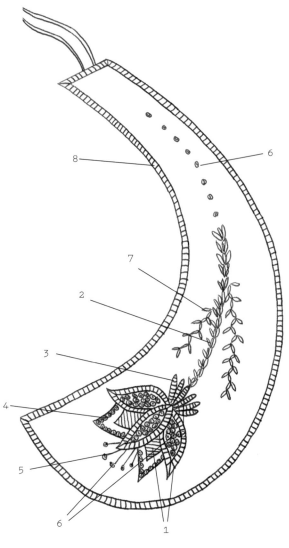

Key

1 Satin stitch
2 Mountmellick stitch
3 Bullion knot
4 Palestrina knot
5 Straight stitch
6 French knot
7 Feather stitch
8 Buttonhole stitch

1 Trace the design template (see p.129) and transfer it to the main fabric (see p.13): centre the satin jean over the design and, using a blue quilter's pencil, make sure you trace both the template outline and floral design (twice, to form both sides of the collar). **Tip:** *If you use a lighter weight fabric, you may need to interface it before stitching. Iron a square on the back of your fabric, big enough to cover the template area.*

2 Mount the fabric in your hoop. Cut a forearm's length of Mountmellick or coton à broder thread and thread into the chenille needle. Tie a knot at one end.

3 Referring to the stitch diagram left, work the motif using the stitches in the following order: **satin stitch, Mountmellick stitch, bullion knots, Palestrina knots, straight stitches, French knots and feather stitch.** With the exception of straight stitch and Mountmellick (see box opposite), all stitches are shown on pp.14-17. Note that the satin stitch and Mountmellick must be worked in opposite directions on the two collars.

4 No line is drawn on the design for **feather stitch,** as you do not want to have a line on the finished design where the stitch does not cover it. You can stitch this by eye or tack (baste) a line in place first, using the sewing needle and sewing thread. After working the feather stitch, remove the tacking stitches.

5 Complete each area of stitching in turn, following the stitch diagram, left. Starting with the knot on the top of the embroidery, take the needle down on your blue line, a short distance away from where you plan to start stitching. Work the stitch back towards the knot on top of the fabric; this will ensure that the trailing thread is caught under the stitches on the back. Once the thread is covered you can cut away the knot. To finish any thread, turn the work over and weave the needle under the stitches on the back. **Tip:** *Keep your hands clean when working with white thread on white fabric. It's good to have a packet of baby wipes on hand!*

5 Once all of the embroidery stitches are complete, remove the fabric from the hoop and press the embroidery face down on a towel, using a cotton setting on your iron.

6 Place your lining fabric face down on a flat surface and the embroidered fabric, face up, on top. With the inner ring of your embroidery hoop lying flat on a work surface, pick up the two pieces of fabric and rest them on top of the hoop with the embroidery facing up. Place the outer hoop on top and push down, fixing the fabric in place.

7 Using your embroidery thread, begin to work the **buttonhole stitch** all the way around the outline of the collar, through both layers of fabric.

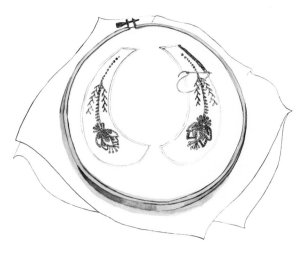

8 The collar can now be cut out. First, using your embroidery scissors, cut the collar out with a 6 mm (¼ in.) allowance all the way around. Then go back around, trimming back to the very edge of the buttonhole stitch, being careful not to cut into the stitches. Use your fingernail to dislodge any loose fibres and trim them away. **Tip:** *Fabric stabilizer spray can be added to the back of buttonhole stitching for added protection.*

Mountmellick stitch

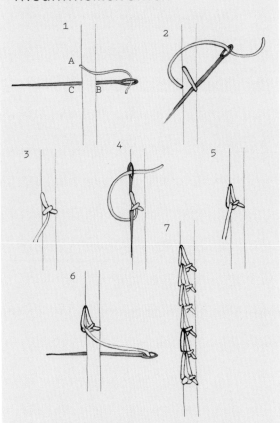

1 Draw or tack (baste) two guidelines on to your fabric a few mm apart. Bring the needle up through the fabric on the left guideline (A). Insert the needle down through the right guideline, a short distance below (B) and out through the left guideline (C).

2 Bring the needle over, and insert it under the first stitch.

3 Pull the thread down to tighten.

4 Insert the needle down through the fabric at the top of the first stitch and out where the second stitch begins, looping the thread under the needle point.

5 Pull the thread down to tighten.

6 Insert the needle down through the right guideline, a short distance below the stitch and out through the left guideline, as in step 1.

7 Repeat steps 2–6 to create an even line of stitches.

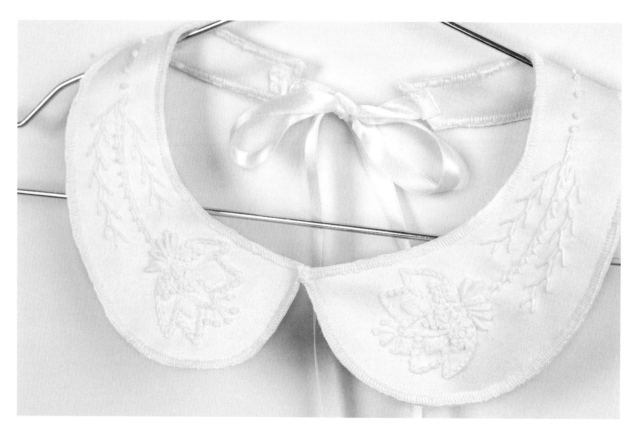

Attach ribbon to each collar piece, and then stitch the two pieces together.

9 Cut your ribbon in half to stitch to either side of the collar. Fold back the end of the first ribbon by 6 mm (¼ in.) and pin the folded side facing the lining, leaving the long end of the ribbon free over the edge of the collar. Using the sewing needle and thread, stitch the ribbon in place with small **slip stitches** (see p.15). Repeat for the other side.

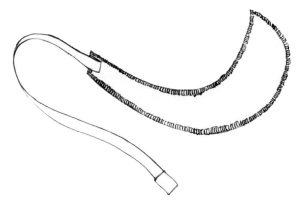

10 So that the ends of the ribbon do not fray, fold them over by 6 mm (¼ in), once then twice, and sew in place.

11 Stitch both of the collar pieces together in the centre at the front, using a straight stitch and Mountmellick thread. Press the collar as in step 5 before wearing.

Now try...

Beads or crystals can be added to the collar (perhaps in place of the French knots) to add sparkle. You can use these same stitches to embellish clothes or accessories; since they work well on heavy, stiff fabric, you can also apply them to curtains or even a lampshade.

Design template

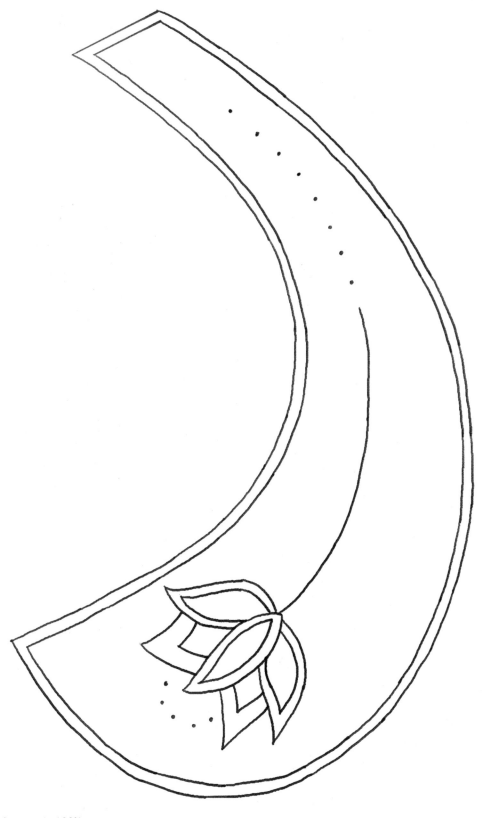

Template shown at 100%

EMBELLISH MENTS

Embellishments are decorative details that enhance and add interest to an embroidery. They can be added after stitching has been done, or they might be integral to the primary design. All manner of ornamentation can be attached – beads and shells and sequins and ribbons. In some cultures, lavishly embroidered, appliquéd and embellished cloths are part of age-old customs and rituals. India has an exceptionally rich heritage of decorated textiles, with techniques including adornment with *shisha* (mirrors) and beetle wings.

Skirt (detail), c.1880
Satin-weave silk embroidered with silk thread and *shisha*,
201 x 86.5 cm (79⅛ x 34 in.)
V&A: IS.2304–1883

SHISHA

'*Shisha* work' is the name given to a form
of embellishment using *shisha* (small mirrors).
Also known as mirror work, it is associated with
the embroidery of western India and Pakistan,
particularly the regions of Saurashtra and Kutch
in Gujarat. Pre-cut discs are often used, but large
pieces of mirror that can be cut into squares,
triangles and other shapes can also be bought.
The pieces of mirror are not pierced but are secured
onto the background fabric using a framework of
stitches, before bright decorative stitching is
worked over this underlying mesh. The base cloth
is further embellished with vivid embroidery, worked
in intricate designs and motifs. *Shisha* mirrors are
now widely available and are a great way to add a
flourish to both modern and traditional designs.

A historical craft

Shisha work has long been used to embellish textiles
of all varieties, from vibrant wall hangings, to
animal trappings, to dress. Communities have often
developed their own distinct styles of design,
passing down motifs from generation to generation.
The craft may have evolved in response to the
availability of naturally occurring mica, but,
from the nineteenth century on, specially made
pieces of mirrored glass were produced. Originally
this glass was blown by hand, but more uniform
factory-manufactured glass is now commonly used.

Boy's tunic, early 20th century
Cotton embroidered with silk
thread and *shisha*, 66 x 87 cm
(26 x 34¼ in.; across sleeves)
V&A: IS.18-1981

Wall hanging, mid-20th century
Cotton embroidered with silk
floss, sequins and *shisha*,
66 x 52 cm (26 x 20½ in.)
V&A: IS.18-1967

Woman's dress, c.1880

Kutch, India, where this dress was made, is a particularly rich area for embroidery; this piece is probably from the Muslim Memon or merchant community in Banni. The garment would have been worn over trousers with matching cuffs, possibly as a wedding dress. Probably made by a professional embroiderer, it is worked in silk thread using buttonhole and interlacing stitch, as well as the chain stitch characteristic of Gujarati embroidery. The contrast of bright thread and mirror with the dark-blue silk ground is particularly arresting.

Satin-weave silk embroidered with silk thread and *shisha*,
111 x 101 cm (43¾ x 39¾ in.)
V&A: IS.2327–1883

CLUTCH BAG

With a palette and design motifs inspired by the dress shown on pp.134–35, this clutch bag is a manageable introduction to the *shisha* technique. Most of the supplies required are readily available, but you may want to do a little research into the different types of *shisha* mirror (see p.138) before you commit!

You will need

Dark-blue cotton sateen/silk with a slight sheen (artificial or natural; the fabric used here is artificial, with a 'slub' like wild silk), 50 cm (20 in.)

Red cotton fabric, for lining, 50 cm (20 in.)

Medium-weight, sew-in interfacing

36 cm (14 in.) zip

DMC stranded cotton (floss): two skeins 712 (ivory), one skein 150 (cherry red), one skein 676 (pale gold), one skein 580 (olive green)

Tacking (basting) thread

General sewing thread, to match both the bag and lining fabric

23 mirrors or mirror sequins, approx. 1.5 cm (⅝ in.) diameter

Hand-sewing needle

Embroidery needle, size 7 or 9

Tracing paper

Dressmaker's carbon paper in orange or yellow

Pen or pencil

Yellow/pale pencil or quilter's pencil

Sewing machine, with standard and zipper feet

Optional
10-12 cm (4-5 in.) embroidery hoop

Project by Caroline Crabtree

How to make

Using different types of *shisha* will produce varying effects.

A note about *shisha*

Handmade *shisha* (above, top right)
The most authentic type of glass *shisha*, and the easiest to use. It is grey-blue, thin and often has small bubbles. It is difficult to find in Western countries, and even in India is getting harder to find.

Machine-cut glass (top middle)
The type that you are most likely to find: pieces of mirror glass cut to shape by machine, 2–3 mm (⅛ in.) thick. The edges are often sharp enough to wear through embroidery thread in time (these are best used with ready-made *shisha* rings). Using a lot of pieces on an item will make it quite heavy.

Mirror sequins (top left and bottom right)
Cheap, readily available, thin, weightless and very easy to use – they have been used for this project. They are easily cut to the required size with scissors, though, for this, you do need sequins without a central hole. As they are plastic, these will buckle and melt if they are pressed with an iron, even on the wrong side.

Ready-made embroidered rings (bottom left)
These are rings of silky embroidery around a plastic ring; place the embroidered ring over the mirror and, with a matching sewing thread, **slip stitch** (see p.15) it into place. Usually supplied with glass or plastic mirror pieces of the appropriate size.

Shisha stitch

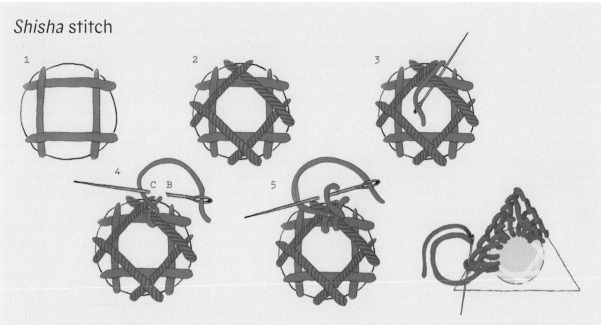

1 Position your *shisha* mirror on the fabric and work an initial frame of four straight stitches to hold it in place.

2 Work a further four stitches diagonally across your frame, as shown. Stitches should be nice and tight.

3 Bring your needle up through the fabric alongside the *shisha* mirror and pass it under the frame stitches, with the thread under the needle as shown.

4 Make a small stitch in the fabric (B–C) as shown, with the thread under the needle again.

5 Repeat steps 3 and 4, working a sort of blanket stitch all around the frame stitches.

6 You can also draw a triangle on to the fabric and use it to shape the stitching, as required.

1 Transfer the bag outline and embroidery design on p.143 onto your outer fabric. First enlarge the template to 100%, then transfer to tracing paper. Sandwich a piece of dressmaker's carbon paper between the traced design and your fabric. Tracing over the design again with the pen or pencil will transfer the lines onto the fabric. **Note:** *The bag outline is the stitching line – you will need to allow an extra 2 cm (¾ in.) for seams all around.*

2 Tack (baste) around the bag outline using a contrasting thread. As you handle the fabric, the carbon line will fade; when it starts to get faint, redraw it using a pale pencil. You may need to do this more than once.

3 Begin to work the embroidery, using an embroidery hoop if you like. Start by cutting a forearm's length of ivory thread. Separate three strands, thread into a needle and knot the end. Work the two semi-circles using **broad chain stitch** (see p.15), 3 mm (⅛ in.) wide, starting from the back of the fabric and using a knot to secure. Using a slightly narrower version of the stitch, work the pointed scallops in green.

Work the chain stitch areas first, before adding the *shisha* pieces.

4   Using two strands of ivory thread, work the spikes on top of each scallop, again using a broad chain stitch, as for the scallops in step 3. Using the same thread and stitch, work the 'X' shapes and flower petals, as shown below.

5   Work the small 'V' shapes in the same way, using broad chain stitch and two strands of green thread.

6   Using three strands of red thread, then pale gold, work broad chain stitch in small semicircles at the base of each flower.

7   Using three strands of red, work **back stitch** (see p.14) around both sides of each of the large semicircles that you stitched in step 3.

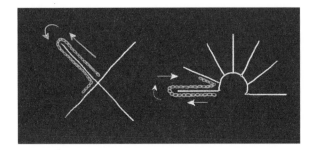

8 Now work the *shisha*, following the stitch diagrams on p.143. Generally, right-handed people work around the *shisha* anticlockwise, and left-handed clockwise. Experiment on some scrap fabric to see which comes more easily to you. Work the circular *shisha* first, using two strands of thread and following the colours in the photograph. **Tip:** *If you are using an embroidery hoop, you will not be able to use it from this point onwards, as the shisha might be crushed by the hoop.*

9 For the *shisha* in the scalloped outline, shape the stitching into a triangle. (You may find it helpful to draw the triangle corners with quilter's pencil.)

10 Finally, using three strands of yellow thread, work backstitch around the four *shisha* in the centre of the design, and the lines around the central *shisha*.

11 To make up the bag, use the template on p.143 to cut two pieces in the lining fabric and two pieces in interfacing, remembering to add a 2 cm (¾ in.) seam allowance to the template.

13 Place lining pieces right sides together. Pin and stitch along the side and bottom edges of the lining, using a 2 cm (¾ in.) seam allowance. Use a thread that matches your lining fabric.

14 Press open the side and bottom seams of the lining, then, at the corners, align the side and base seam and stitch across the corner (see illustration below). Turn the lining right side out and press a 2 cm (¾ in.) hem to the wrong side around the top edge. Top stitch around this edge, to hold the hem in place.

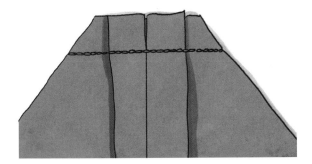

15 Change to a dark-blue sewing thread to match your outer fabric and attach the zipper foot to your sewing machine.

16 Pin the embroidered fabric piece to one of your interfacing pieces, and do the same for the plain back piece of the bag. You will treat fabric and interfacing as one layer in the following steps.

17 Place front and back right sides together and tack along the top edges. Open the seam out flat and, on the wrong side, centre your zip over the seam. Using the zipper foot on your machine, stitch each along side of the zip, 4 mm (⅛ in.) from the tacked seam. You may need to open the zip a little, make a few stitches, lift your foot to close the zip and then lower it and continue, to get round the zip pull.

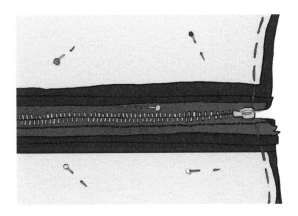

18 Remove the tacking stitches and check that your zip will open and close. Open the zip and, at the open end, turn under the seam allowance of the bag edge and zip tape, and **slip stitch** (see p.15) in place. Close the zip.

19 With right sides together again, stitch both side seams of the bag, though all layers of fabric, including the fold of the zip and seam allowance at the top edge.

20 Open the zip and stitch the bottom seam of the bag; as you did with the lining in step 14, open the side and base seams flat and stitch the corners. You can remove the pins holding the interfacing in place at this point.

21 Keeping the bag inside out, place the lining, right side out, over the bag. Slip stitch the lining in place around the top edge of the bag, stitching into the edge of the zip tape (don't stitch too close to the zip itself). Turn the bag right side out to finish.

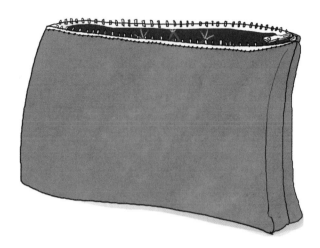

Now try...

Adapting this design for a cushion motif, by tracing the design and then flipping it and re-tracing to complete the oval design. See pp.105–6 for instructions on constructing a basic cushion.

Design template

Template shown at 50%

BEETLE WING

The ancient craft of the application of iridescent beetle wings to artwork has traditionally been practised in India, Japan, Myanmar (Burma) and Thailand. In India, dazzling textiles decorated with beetle wings, most commonly in emerald hues, along with other sparkling embellishments, survive from the seventeenth century onwards. In the nineteenth and early-twentieth centuries, fashionable Western women also wore gowns adorned with shimmering beetle-wing embroidery. The wings were pierced and stitched onto fabric, frequently imitating floral designs.

A natural embellishment

These lustrous ornamentations are actually the beetle's protective wing casing (*elytra*), though they are commonly referred to as wings. Naturally shed as part of the beetle's life cycle, they are collected from some of the larger and more eye-catching specimens of the *Buprestidae* family, also known as jewel beetles or metallic wood-boring beetles. The wings are highly valued for their glowing and long-lasting colours, created by the microscopic structure of the wing, not by its pigmentation. Relatively hard and durable, provided they are treated with care, it's not unusual for these jewel-like decorations to outlast the textiles to which they have been attached.

Border for a woman's dress, 19th century

The dazzling effect of this textile – presumably even more dazzling when in motion – has been achieved through the application of beetle wings to plain-woven muslin, with each wing standing in for a leaf in the naturalistic designs arranged along the border. This kind of decoration is often used only for the borders of dress, as here, to minimize crushing, as the wings themselves, though durable, are brittle, and fracture under pressure. The technique was especially popular in mid-nineteenth- and early-twentieth-century Europe, having been used in indigenous Indian and Mughal court dress.

Muslin embroidered with beetle wings and gold wire,
117 x 33 cm (46 x 13 in.)
V&A: IS.468–1992

HANGING EMBROIDERY

In nineteenth-century India, Western women were exposed to traditional embroidered textiles featuring beetle-wing pieces, and these were incorporated into their (otherwise Western-style) dress. Our project draws inspiration from both Indian-made textiles (see the object on p.145) and their Western applications. This sampler is a lovely decoration and would make a beautiful gift!

You will need

Cream-coloured muslin (gauze fabric), 28 x 28 cm (11 x 11 in.)
White cotton (for backing), 28 x 28 cm (11 x 11 in.)
Display frame of your choice
White felt, approx. 18 cm (7 in.) square
1 skein DMC Metallic Pearl thread, 5282 (gold)
1 skein DMC Light Effects embroidery thread, E699 (green)
Couching thread, DMC Diamant: one skein green; one skein gold
Buttonhole thread, white
5 beetle wings with 2 holes: 2 x large, 2 x medium, 1 x small
3 beetle wings of any size (to be cut down)
25 3 mm (⅛ in.) green sequins
25 gold sequins or spangles, same size or slightly smaller than green sequins
Embroidery/crewel needle, sizes 5 and 10
Hand-sewing needle, sharps 9
Sharp pencil or washable marker of your choice
Embroidery, or other sharp, fine-pointed scissors
18 cm (7 in.) embroidery hoop

Project by Sarah Homfray

How to make

1 Trace the design template (see p.151) and transfer to your fabric, as follows. Position your cotton backing fabric over the design (keeping the design central and square with the fabric) and trace the design using a sharp pencil or marker of your choice. **Tip:** *If you can't see the design very well through the fabric, trace over it with a black pen to make it stand out more.*

2 Place the muslin over the backing fabric and secure both in the embroidery hoop. Check that the design shows through.

3 Sort your five beetle wings to fit the pattern: place larger ones at the bottom of the design and the smallest at the point.

4 Cut out some small round pieces from the remaining wings using your embroidery scissors; cut the wings into three pieces, then round off the edges with the scissors. Now use a small needle to make holes in the centre of each piece for sewing down; support the wing from underneath (pad with a piece of absorbent cotton, fabric or similar) and carefully make a small hole – you can make it larger by taking the whole needle through.

5 Cut a forearm's length of the gold couching thread and thread into the size 10 embroidery needle. Stitch all the wings in place, starting with the bottom wings. Tie a knot in one end of the thread and take the needle down through the fabric on one of the design lines. Work two small stitches close to the knot to secure the end of the thread and then work a single stitch from the edge of the wing down into the hole in the centre; repeat for all of the wings. Do the same for the second bottom wing, then stitch on the next two and finally the one on the tip. Just putting in one stitch at this stage will allow you to adjust the angles of the wings in relation to each other.

6 Once all the wings are in place, work more stitches around each wing as shown in the illustration below, always coming up on the outside of the wing and down into the hole. When you have finished the stitching, you can cut off your starting knots.

Begin by stitching the five large wings in place.

7 Again using the gold couching thread, stitch the small round cut pieces of wing in place using the same method – work three stitches coming up from the outside of each piece and down into the hole.

8 Couch down the gold Metallic Pearl thread around the inner teardrop-shaped border. Cut about 55 cm (22 in.) of the gold thread, fold it in half and work your first **couching** stitch (see p.16) over the fold at the bottom of the shape, using the green Diamant thread. Couch over the now-doubled gold thread with the green, working all around the shape and spacing the stitches about 5 mm (¼ in.) apart. When you reach the top, stitch each gold thread down individually to obtain a nice sharp point.

9 Fasten off the threads. Thread the gold ends through the size 5 embroidery needle and take through to the back of the fabric. Take the green thread through also and use this to sew down the ends. Sew over about 1 cm (⅜ in.) in the backing fabric only, secure the end of the green thread and cut off all excess thread.

10 Using a single gold Metallic Pearl thread, work around the lower left wing and the lower right wing, couching in the same way as before. When you reach the bottom of a wing, stitch the gold next to the first piece to create a stem. Fasten off threads. Repeat for the middle pair of wings, working a stem at the end that joins up with the wings below. Repeat again for the final wing, at the top of the design.

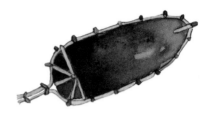

11 Again using couching, work a single length (approx. 130 cm/50 in.) of gold Metallic Pearl around the decorative, looped outside shape. Couch down with gold couching thread. Start from the point and form a loop of thread on each peak. Work a couching stitch between each loop and at the top and bottom of the loops. Work your way around the shape and back to the starting point. Take both threads through to the back at the point and fasten off on the back as before, using the gold couching thread to sew the ends down.

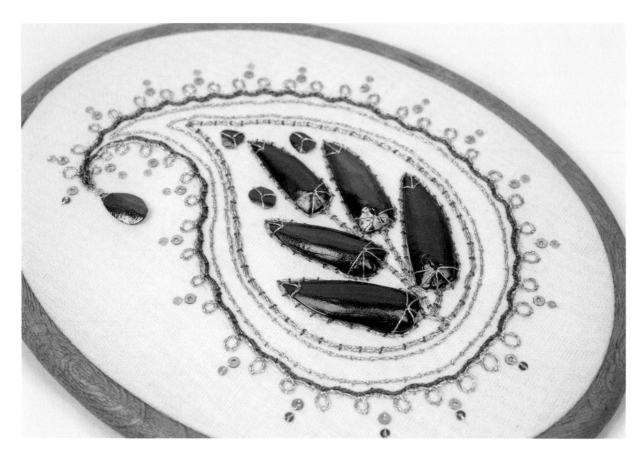

Complete the couched borders before finishing with a final beetle-wing piece and the sequins.

12 Work a second row of couching inside the looped row using the green Light Effects thread and couching down with the green Diamant thread. Follow the curves of the looped row, placing the green row up tight against it (as shown above).

13 Work two separate rows of couching between the green row and the inner tear drop outline, leaving a gap between the rows, as indicated on the design template. Use a single length of the gold Metallic Pearl for these and couch down with the gold Diamant thread.

14 Cut a teardrop-shaped beetle wing, make a small hole near its point and sew in place on the top point of the shape, as pictured above.

15 Sew down the sequins; start with the green, using the green couching thread. Bring the needle up on a dot and thread on the sequin. Make a stitch over the edge of the sequin and back up into the middle again. Make a second stitch opposite the first before tying off. Next, sew on the gold sequins or spangles above the green ones, this time using the gold couching thread to sew them down.

16 Place the display frame over the felt and draw around the inside of it. Next, remove your embroidery from the hoop and centre the frame over it. Holding the frame in place, draw a line about 4 cm (1½ in.) away from it, all the way around, then cut away the excess muslin and backing along this line.

17 Thread a length of buttonhole thread in the larger embroidery needle and work a large **running stitch** (see p.14) 1.5 cm (⅝ in.) from the edge of the fabric, all the way around. Pull on the ends of the thread to gather this excess fabric to the back of the frame and secure the end of the thread.

18 Cut out the oval shape from the piece of felt and pin in place. **Slip stitch** (see p.15) to the back of the embroidery and remove pins to finish.

Now try...

If you're not comfortable sewing with beetle wings, or would just like to try a different effect, try using acrylic fingernails instead! They are easily available and come in lots of different sizes and colours; you can even re-paint them in your own colours and designs.

Design template

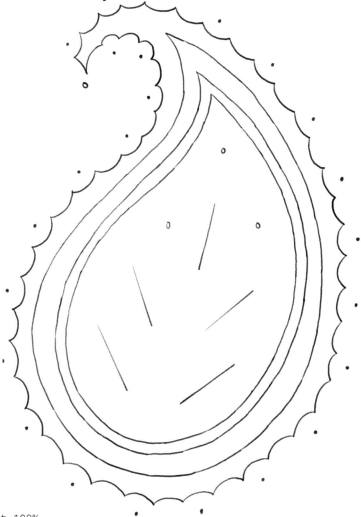

Template shown at 100%

AINU APPLIQUÉ

Ainu appliqué is a form of onlay embroidered appliqué practised by the Ainu people of Hokkaido, the northernmost island of Japan. Onlay appliqué is the technique of applying fabric shapes onto a background cloth; bold and dramatic patterns can be created relatively quickly with minimal stitching required. The Ainu decorate their dress with navy or black ribbon-like strips of cotton appliquéd in pre-planned patterns onto the brown background fabric, in a process called *kirifuse*. The motifs are secured in place with stitching that matches the appliqué material. The designs are then further embellished with couched (laid) white cotton threads in a method known as *oki nui*; stem stitch and chain stitch are also sometimes used.

Significant design

The Ainu are indigenous to Hokkaido and have their own language, religion, culture and costumes, different from those of the Japanese. The best-known garment from this culture is a robe called an *attush*, which is made from cloth woven from the inner bark fibres of an elm native to Hokkaido. Worn by a man conducting one of many religious rituals belonging to the Ainu culture, such a robe was always made and decorated by women. The embroidered cotton appliqué around the necks, hems and sleeves of the robe was worked in very specific designs, such as *moreu* (spirals) and *aiushi* (thorns), passed from mother to daughter.

Robe, pre-1910
Cotton embroidered and with
wool appliqué, 50.8 x 61 cm
(20 x 24 in.; across sleeves)
V&A: T.264-1910

Robe, mid-19th century

The 'thorn-like' appliquéd cotton patterns on this Ainu robe, and the accompanying couched thread designs, reflect their traditional role as a form of protection against malevolent spirits. This *attush* is made of bark fibre, from either the *Ulmus laciniata* or *Tilia iaponica* species, and has a simple construction, consisting of four straight pieces of cloth seamed at the back and sides, with two straight pieces attached as sleeves. A paper-stiffened collar and black knotted cords, acting as fastenings, are the only other elements in the garment's construction.

Ohyo (elm-bark fibre) embroidered with cotton and with cotton appliqué, 128.5 x 128 cm (52.5 x 50 in.; across shoulders and sleeves)
V&A: T.99–1963

THORN-PATTERN BAG

The top of this bag features the characteristic 'thorn' pattern of Ainu appliqué. Ainu clothing was traditionally made from fibres including elm bark and nettles, so choose a fabric with natural look for your bag. The appliqué is worked by hand, using the needleturn method, but the bag can be made using sewing-machine techniques if preferred (see 'Now Try').

You will need

Neutral cotton or linen fabric, for bag construction:
Bag panel: 86 x 33 cm (34 x 13 in.)
Handles: two pieces, each 10 x 35.5 cm (4 x 14 in.)

Dark-blue cotton fabric, for appliqué and lining:
Lining: 86 x 33 cm (34 x 13 in.)
Edging: two strips, each 4.5 x 33 cm (1¾ x 13 in.
Appliqué motif: 34 x 18 cm (13¼ x 7 in.; or double this if you want the motif on both sides of the bag)

General sewing thread to match both fabrics (a fine thread is best for appliqué)

Tacking (basting) thread

One skein coton à broder or cotton perlé, no.12, beige or cream

Sharps or appliqué needle, size 9 or 10

Embroidery needle, suitable for thread chosen

Tracing paper

Pen or pencil

Pins

Japanese *chaco* (chalk transfer) paper or dressmaker's carbon paper

Erasable marker, suitable for dark fabrics

Sewing machine and general sewing threads as above

Project by Susan Briscoe

How to make

1 Trace or photocopy the appliqué design template on p.161 and transfer it to your appliqué fabric using either a lightbox/window and an erasable marker, or Japanese *chaco* paper/dressmaker's carbon paper (see p.13). **Note:** *Remember that this is a half-pattern and will need to be flipped and retraced to transfer the full, symmetrical design.* If using *chaco* paper, place the design template over the appliqué fabric and pin in place. Slide the *chaco* paper under the template, coloured side down, and, on a hard surface, trace around the template lines using a ballpoint pen. Check that the design has transferred and that you have gone over all lines before removing pins.

2 Trace or photocopy the template for the bag edging; you will use this in step 4.

3 Next, prepare to stitch the appliqué. First, use your sewing machine and zig-zag all around the edge of the bag panel, so that it does not fray as you work.

4 Now take your edging strips and turn under a 6 mm (¼ in.) hem allowance along one long side of each. Press. Transfer the relevant part of the embroidery pattern (see step 2) onto one strip, aligning the bottom of the edging template with the fold. **Note:** *Remember that this is a half-pattern and will need to be flipped and retraced to transfer the full, symmetrical design.*

5 Place the marked edging strips together with your bag panel, right sides facing out, lining up the raw edge of each edging strip with each short end of the bag panel. Pin and tack. Machine stitch, using a zigzag, or overlock, the top and raw edges of each strip to the bag panel (this will be hidden later). Now appliqué the lower, folded edge of each strip to the bag panel (see needle-turn appliqué tips opposite).

6 Carefully cut out the appliqué along the dashed lines, which allow a 3 mm (⅛ in.) hem allowance around all the motifs. Do not clip into curves or right angles just yet - wait until you are about to stitch these sections, to avoid unnecessary fraying. Pin the appliqué to the right side of the 'front' of your bag panel, aligning the upper edge with the seam of the edging strip and front panel, and tack (baste) all round the appliqué, 6 mm (¼ in.) from the edges, with fairly short stitches. The tacking is essential and will keep your appliqué even in the next step.

7 You are now ready to begin sewing the appliqué motifs to the bag panel. The needleturn method gives a firm, strong and neat edge to the appliquéd shapes. Start and finish sewing at the sides of the appliqué motif, with a small knot and a few tiny **running stitches** (see p.14) hidden under the edge of the appliqué. (Do not turn under the appliqué right at the sides of the bag, as these edges will disappear into the side seams later). Use an appliqué, or a long sharps needle to turn under the raw edge a little at a time as you sew, as shown in the illustration below. Press the turned edge with your fingers, come up through the folded edge of the appliqué shape with your needle and stitch back down into the backing fabric. Repeat, keeping the stitches at right angles to the folded edge on top of your work, as this makes them almost invisible. Create sharp points and corners by leaving the previous couple of stitches loose, pushing the point of the fabric under the shape as far as possible and then gently tightening up the sewing thread. The loose stitches will tighten up and the point will pull out perfectly. **Note:** *It is not necessary to clip the fabric around outer curves and corners; just ease it under. Only the right angle and curved inner corner shapes need clipping.*

8 The **stem stitch** (see p.14) embroidery is worked as several long continuous lines that meander across the appliqué, which can be worked in any order you like. Each 'point' is stitched slightly over the edge of the appliquéd motifs, into the background fabric. There are several points where the stem stitch overlaps a previous line. When you have finished, press the work lightly.

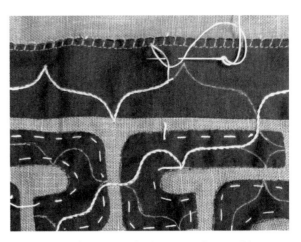

Stem stitch is worked in long continuous lines over the appliqué.

9 Construct the bag handles from your two fabric pieces. Fold and press each handle as shown in the illustration below, and then machine sew along both long edges of each handle, about 2 mm (¹⁄₁₆ in.) from the edge.

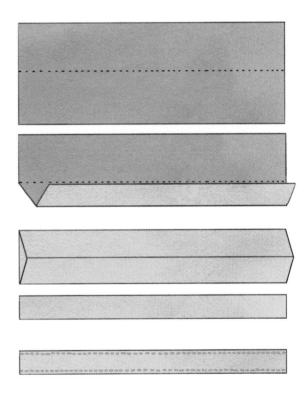

10 With the bag panel folded in half, right sides together, and using a 1 cm (⅜ in.) seam, machine sew down the sides of the bag using a straight stitch. **Note:** *Start and finish all construction seams with a few backstitches to secure your threads.*

11 Make the lining by folding your lining fabric in half, right sides together and, again with a 1 cm (⅜ in.) seam, machine sew down both sides, leaving a 10 cm (4 in.) gap unsewn in the second side. Press the bag and lining side seams to one side, in such a way that they will be facing in opposite directions when the lining is sewn into the bag.

12 Keep your outer bag section turned inside out and position the handles, one on each side, so that the raw ends overlap the edge of the bag panel by 1.3 cm (½ in.). The gap between the handle ends is 7.5 cm (3 in.) on each side. Make sure the handles are the same length, in the same position on each side of the bag, and not twisted. Tack (baste) in place.

13 Keeping the bag lining turned inside out, place the bag outer inside it, lining up the top edge and the side seams. Machine sew all around the top of the bag with a 1 cm (⅜ in.) seam. Turn the bag right side out, through the unsewn gap in the lining side seam. Press. For a neat, secure finish, hand sew around the inside of the top of the bag, about 3 mm (⅛ in.) from the edge, taking small stitches through the lining and the seam allowance only, without letting your stitches show on the outside of the bag. Turn the bag inside out and **slip stitch** (see p.15) the gap in the lining closed.

Your finished bag will be fully lined, with the handle ends concealed inside.

Now try...

Bonded appliqué, stitched and embroidered by machine. First iron your appliqué motif onto a bonding material, then cut out, without the seam allowance. Iron the motif to the panel at the temperature advised by the manufacturer and machine sew around the edge using using a narrow, slightly open zigzag or a blanket stitch. The embroidered line can be stitched with a heavier machine thread, such as a no.12 weight.

Bag edging template (top) and appliqué design template (below)

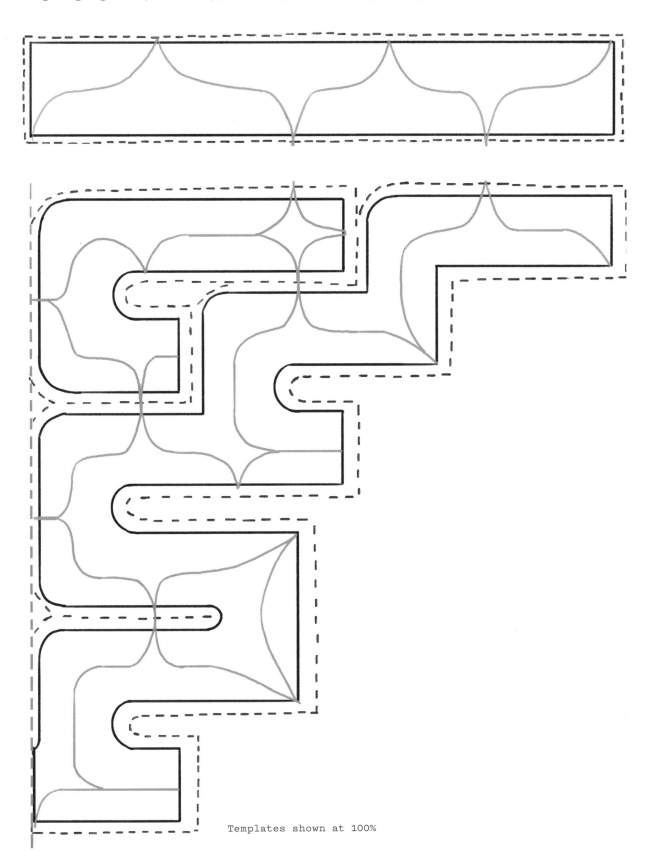

Templates shown at 100%

CONTEMPORARY

Today's embroiderer has an enormous range of methods and materials at their disposal. Long-established techniques such as couching and drawn-thread work can be executed by hand or machine, and pre-programmed designs and free-machine embroidery have opened up a whole new world of creative needlework. In addition to traditional cloths, there is a host of new fabrics, including soluble backgrounds, which can be dissolved away after stitching to make lacy, ethereal pieces, such as those by Meredith Woolnough (p.165). A plethora of threads for both hand and machine stitching allow a wide variety of textures and effects to be produced. Unorthodox, recycled and reclaimed materials can also be used to make inventive mixed-media work.

Rebecca Crompton, 'Fantasy' panel, 1936–37
Silver-gilt fabric with machine embroidery, 56 x 43 cm (22 x 16⅞ in.)
V&A: CIRC.217–1948

EMBROIDERY

DRAWING WITH THREAD

Using needle and thread as one would a pencil or brush, basic hand stitches, such as running or backstitch, can be used to 'draw' or 'paint' pictorial or abstract designs onto a surface. Sketch-like images can be created from simple outline 'doodles', with decorative stitches, embellishments or snippets of fabric used to add accents. Dense stitching in a range of tints and tones can also produce wonderful, painterly effects. Thread drawing and painting can also be worked using free-machine embroidery, which employs just a simple straight stitch, with more elaborate stitches, like zigzag, used to add further texture.

Free-machine embroidery
In normal machine stitching, fabric is held between the presser foot and the teeth of the feed dogs; the up-and-down motion of the dogs 'feeds' the fabric under the needle. In free-machine embroidery, the feed dogs are dropped and the machine's operator has complete control over the movement of the fabric. The range of designs and patterns that can be created is limited only by the embroiderer's imagination. This technique takes time to master, but there are simple tips and tricks that help, including the use of a hoop to keep fabric taut and stable, and investing in a darning or open-toe foot, so that you can see where you have just stitched!

Meredith Woolnough, *Maple Branch*, **2015**
Embroidery thread and pins on paper,
62 x 75 cm (24⅜ x 29½ in.)
Private collection

James Merry, *Adidas/Strawberry*, **2016**
Vintage sportswear with embroidery,
Embroidered area: 20 x 15 cm
(7⅞ x 5⅞ in.)
Private collection

Evening dress, 1940

Elsa Schiaparelli, though made famous by more unconventional designs, was also a master of the simple black dress. She herself wore this fluid, black crêpe creation. Its simple, elegant shape is enlivened by a bold area of embroidery executed by Lesage, a company closely associated with Schiaparelli, which still operates today, creating specialist work for couture houses including Chanel. The lily motif (which inspired the project overleaf) has been created using pearls of various sizes, sequins and gilt metallic strip. It is an example of the high-quality pictorial embroidery often executed by hand for couture houses of the twentieth century.

Silk crêpe, embroidered with pearls, sequins,
metal strip and plastic, 148.5 x 74.5 cm (58½ x 29⅜ in.)
V&A: T.48–1965

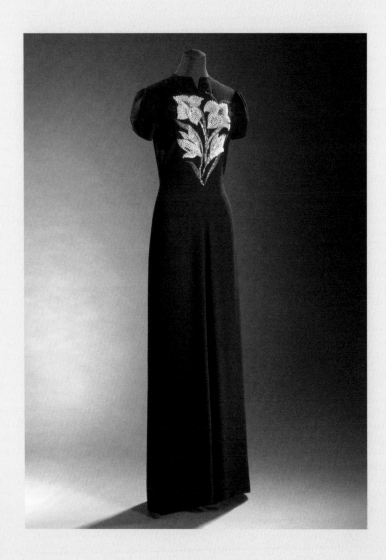

FLORAL-MOTIF LINGERIE

You can consider this technique a way of 'drawing with stitch', using the sewing machine as you would a pencil or pen. The instructions on the following pages show you how to embellish a pair of black French knickers with a lily motif, inspired by the gown shown on pp.166–67; you can, however, use the same technique to sew any design, including those you draft yourself.

You will need

Base fabric: a dress, piece of lingerie or loose fabric (avoid stretch fabrics until you are feeling more confident with the technique)

Dissolvable/water-soluble fabric

Machine embroidery threads (polyester/cotton mix or 100% polyester), colours to suit your design including a bobbin thread in a neutral or fabric-matching shade

Sewing machine with darning foot

Ballpoint pen and pencil

Dressmaker's carbon paper

20 cm (8 in.) embroidery hoop

Project by Naomi Ryder

How to make

1 Sketch your design on a piece of paper, or use the design template provided opposite.

2 Place a piece of dressmaker's carbon paper on the right side of your fabric, with the coloured, carbon, side facing down. Place your design on top of the paper, and draw over the design lines using a ballpoint pen to transfer the image onto the fabric.

3 Cut a piece of dissolvable fabric, around 30 cm (12 in.) square. Place this underneath your garment and place both, face up, over the outer ring of the hoop. Push the inner ring down over the fabric and outer hoop. If your fabric is delicate, wrap the hoop first (see p.11). The dissolvable fabric will act as a stabilizer. **Tip:** *Make sure the fabric is very taut in the hoop at all times.*

4 Thread your machine with a neutral-coloured bobbin thread (or a colour that matches your fabric) and a top thread in the colour of your choice. Drop the feed dogs on your machine, to allow you to control the fabric movement and direction of sewing once you get started. Use the darning foot.

5 Set a medium-length straight stitch and position the fabric under the foot at your starting point. (You may find it easiest to start in the middle of the design and work your way out.) Lower the presser foot, then lower the needle into the fabric. Holding on to both top and bobbin threads (to prevent the machine from 'eating' your fabric), stitch one or two stitches forwards, then backwards, then forwards again, to secure the stitching (repeat when fastening off). Now begin stitching over the design lines.

6 Continue to stitch over your design lines. Don't be shy about changing your top thread to make your design come to life – work as if you were drawing or painting!

7 When you have finished stitching the design, cut off all the loose ends close to the fabric. Remove the hoop, and on the wrong side, trim the dissolvable fabric around the design to remove any excess.

8 Rinse your fabric/garment in cool water, or otherwise follow product instructions to remove the dissolvable fabric. Rinse, then dry and press carefully.

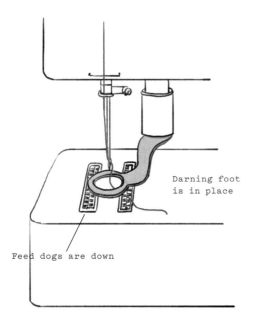

Darning foot is in place

Feed dogs are down

Now try...

Your own design. And you're not limited to flowers! You can transform any graphic into a drawing with thread with a bit of practice: portraits, patterns, or even words and lettering.

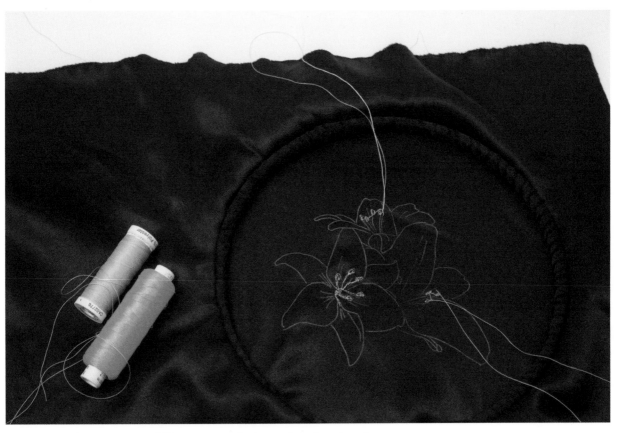

Start stitching from the middle of your design and work outwards.

Design template

Template shown at 100%

ABOUT THE MAKERS

Lucy Barter

Lucy Barter holds a BA Honours in fashion design and spent several years designing for established children's labels in the UK and the US. She then discovered the Royal School of Needlework (RSN) and was inspired to enrol in the RSN's three-year apprenticeship programme. After graduating in August 2006, Barter moved to San Francisco, where she taught for the RSN for many years, while also running her own business, Forever Embroidery Studio. In 2015, Lucy co-founded the San Francisco School of Needlework and Design, where she also teaches and encourages everyone to try needlework.
www.foreverembroiderystudio.com/
www.sfsnad.org

Susan Briscoe

Susan Briscoe lives in Perthshire, Scotland, where she teaches patchwork, *sashiko* quilting and creative textile design, and writes and designs for a variety of patchwork and needlecraft magazines. She is the author of a number of practical books on Japanese textile traditions, including *The Ultimate Sashiko Sourcebook: Patterns, Projects and Inspirations* (2005), *Japanese Quilt Inspirations* (2011) and *Japanese Quilt Blocks to Mix and Match* (2007).
www.susanbriscoe.com

Caroline Crabtree

Caroline Crabtree began sewing at a young age. She was an apprentice at the Royal School of Needlework (RSN) before embarking on self-employment, with a mixture of design, restoration, and new work. She pursued an increasing interest in global embroidery, costume and household textiles, leading to the publication of her first book, *World Embroidery* (1993), followed by *Patchwork*, *Appliqué and Quilting* (2007) and *Beadwork: A World Guide* (2009), both co-authored. She (mostly) retired from travelling and teaching in 2002.

Rachel Doyle

A freelance embroiderer, designer and tutor in hand embroidery, Rachel Doyle has a degree in textiles and also trained for three years at the Royal School of Needlework (RSN). As a graduate apprentice of the RSN, Doyle now teaches for the School as well as working in their commercial studio. She has worked on a variety of conservation and restoration projects, as well as new commissions including the wedding dress and veil of the Duchess of Cambridge. She is the author of *Canvaswork* in the RSN Essential Stitch Guide series.
www.racheldoyle.studio

Sarah Homfray

Sarah Homfray trained on the prestigious three-year Royal School of Needlework Apprenticeship, graduating in 2006. She has also gained a Certificate in Education, and a Diploma in Fine Art from the Cyprus College of Art. She has taught across the UK and US and is privileged to have been part of the team of embroiderers who worked on the wedding dress of the Duchess of Cambridge in 2011, and to have made the replica standard of the 105th Regiment for the Waterloo 200 anniversary commemorations. Homfray now works from her studio in Nottinghamshire, teaching and running her online embroidery shop.
www.sarahhomfray.com
@sarahhomfray

Dr Lynn Hulse

Lynn Hulse is a Visiting Research Fellow at the V&A, specializing in art embroidery in the home, c.1860–1914. A former archivist at the Royal School of Needlework, she is also a Trustee of the Brangwyn Gift at the William Morris Gallery, Fellow of the Society of Antiquaries of London and co-founder of Ornamental Embroidery, which teaches and designs historic handmade embroidery inspired by objects from museum and private collections. She is the editor of *May Morris: New Perspectives. Proceedings of the May Morris Conference Held at the William Morris Gallery*, May 2016 (Friends of the William Morris Gallery, 2017).
www.ornamentalembroidery.com

Naomi Ryder

Award-winning textile designer and illustrator Naomi Ryder utilizes embroidery, drawing with stitch to create delicate contemporary images of everyday life. Ryder's 'Out of the Ordinary' stationery collection features themes including British birds, London architecture and the 'girls' night out'. Ryder has been illustrating on commission for many years: previous clients have included the V&A, Southbank Centre and retail consultant Mary Portas.
www.naomiryder.co.uk
@Naomiryder

INDEX

Picture credits

7 left: courtesy Meredith Woolnough

7 above: courtesy James Merry

7 below right: Santiago Felipe/Getty Images

8 above left: courtesy Tessa Perlow

8 above right: courtesy Tirelli Costumi

8 below: Francois Durand/Getty Images

9 above: courtesy Fine Cell Work

9 below left: Kay-Paris Fernandes/Getty Images

9 below right: Victor Virgile/Gamma-Rapho via Getty Images

21: courtesy Susan Briscoe

97: courtesy William Morris Society

121: courtesy Marèe Maher

165 above: courtesy Meredith Woolnough

165 below: courtesy James Merry

166, 167: courtesy Schiaparelli

Acknowledgments

The publishers would like to thank Anne Williams, who compiled the historical texts in this book. Our thanks also go to the V&A curators who read and advised on the historical texts: Clare Browne, Sau Fong Chan, Avalon Fotheringham, Anna Jackson, Rosalie Kim, Divia Patel and Josephine Rout.

DMC threads are available from DMC stockists throughout the UK and internationally. Please visit www.dmccreative.co.uk or www.dmc.com for more information.

We would love to see what you create! Share your pictures online using the hashtag #vamMakers